MUSIC IN THE CASTLE

RENEWALS 691-4574

DATE DUE

F. ALBERTO GALLO

MUSIC
IN THE CASTLE

*Troubadours, Books, and Orators
in Italian Courts of the
Thirteenth, Fourteenth, and
Fifteenth Centuries*

*Translated from the Italian by
Anna Herklotz*

*Translations from Latin by
Kathryn Krug*

THE UNIVERSITY OF CHICAGO PRESS
Chicago & London

F. ALBERTO GALLO is professor of medieval and renaissance
music at the University of Bologna.

The University of Chicago Press, Chicago 60637
The University of Chicago Press, Ltd., London
©1995 by The University of Chicago
All rights reserved. Published 1995
Printed in the United States of America
04 03 02 01 00 99 98 97 96 95   1 2 3 4 5

ISBN: 0-226-27968-5 (cloth)
0-226-27969-3 (paper)
Originally published as *Musica nel castello: Trovatori, libri,
oratori nelle corti italiane dal XIII al XV secolo,*
©1992 Società editrice Il Mulino, Bologna

Gallo, F. Alberto.
    [Musica nel castello. English]
    Music in the castle : troubadours, books, and orators in
Italian courts of the thirteenth, fourteenth, and fifteenth cen-
turies / F. Alberto Gallo : translated from the Italian by Anna
Herklotz : translations from Latin by Kathryn Krug.
        p.   cm.
    Translation of : Musica nel castello.
    Includes bibliographical references and index.
    1.   Music—Italy—500–1400—History and criticism.
I. Herklotz, Anna.   II. Krug, Kathryn.
ML290.2.G313   1995
780'.945'0902—dc20   95–9257
                                                                CIP
                                                                MN

The paper used in this publication meets the minimum
requirements of the American National Standard
for Information Sciences—Permanence of Paper
for Printed Library Materials, ANSI Z39.48-1984.

Contents

Introduction

When in 1988 I was invited to Harvard University for a period of teaching and research (under the auspices of the Lauro De Bosis Committee[1] and the Department of Music[2]), one of my responsibilities was to give three public lectures. As I contemplated possible subjects for these lectures I found that a general focus was easy enough to establish, since it seemed only natural that I should dedicate one lecture to each of the three centuries—thirteenth, fourteenth, and fifteenth—in which I most commonly concentrate my research. Selecting specific topics within each century was, however, a much more difficult task, because my audience would comprise not just musicologists but also individuals with a general interest in Italian cultural history; and it is widely recognized that musicology and the history of culture normally have little in common, which is to say each largely ignores the other. For this reason I chose three areas where the lack of interaction between musicological endeavors and research in other historical-cultural areas is particularly striking, so that the attempt to establish a connection between them might prove equally interesting.

Musicological studies on the troubadours have always addressed technical problems (philological assessments, formal classifications, research

---

1   Composed of my colleagues Dante Della Terza, Mason Hammond, and Lewis Lockwood, whom I wish to thank here.
2   Whose members I wish to thank as well, particularly Christoph Wolff, then acting chairman, and again Lewis Lockwood, with whom I presented a joint seminar on music of the Quattrocento.

into performance practice),[3] never historical, social, or cultural questions; consequently they lend scant attention to the activity of troubadours in Italian courts. And though this activity has been studied at length by literary historians, they seem to have entirely ignored the existence of any music for the poetic texts.[4]

Music at the Visconti court has been examined extensively, especially in recent years;[5] but researchers have been more concerned with establishing the provenance and whereabouts of individual works and composers than with studying this music's relation to daily life, to general artistic interests, or to other cultural initiatives at court. Conversely, not even the most complete and detailed work on the political and cultural history of the Visconti dynasty gives any space to musical activity.[6]

Finally, musicological inquiry regarding the Italian Quattrocento—ranging from the general European overview of music to the investigation of a specific court, for example Ferrara or Naples[7]—has been solely concerned with professional musicians. It therefore ignores the interests and musical practices of an entire category of cultured people, the *oratores* (commonly blurred by the modern and ambiguous label of "humanists"), such as Aurelio Brandolini or Ludovico Carboni. Historical-literary studies of these individuals and their cultural milieu, on the other hand, make no reference whatsoever to their music.[8]

---

3 See Theodore Karp, "Troubadours, Trouvères," in *The New Grove Dictionary of Music and Musicians,* vol. 19 (London, 1980), pp. 196–208; Karp summarizes the results of musicological studies in four areas: manuscript sources, modality, form, and rhythm.

4 From such general overviews as that of Alfred Jeanroy, *La poésie lyrique des troubadours,* vol. 1 (Toulouse and Paris, 1934), pp. 229–65, and Aurelio Roncaglia, "Le corti medievali," in *Letteratura italiana,* ed. Alberto Asor Rosa, vol. 1 (Turin, 1982), pp. 107–22, to specialized studies such as those cited in notes 2 and 32 to chapter 1.

5 Geneviève Thibault, "Emblèmes et devises des Visconti dans les oeuvres musicales du Trecento," in *L'ars nova italiana del Trecento,* vol. 3 (Certaldo, 1970), pp. 131–60; F. Alberto Gallo, *La polifonia nel Medioevo* (Turin, 1991), pp. 65–69 (English edition, *Music of the Middle Ages II* [Cambridge, 1985], pp. 59–60); Reinhard Strohm, "Filippotto da Caserta, ovvero I Francesi in Lombardia," in *In cantu et in sermone: A Nino Pirrotta nel suo 80° compleanno* (Florence, 1989), pp. 65–74; and *The Lucca Codex,* ed. John Nádas and Agostino Ziino (Lucca, 1990), pp. 35–45.

6 One striking example is the case of the monumental *Storia di Milano,* 16 vols. (Milan, 1953–62), in which the first chapter on musical activity appears in the volume dealing with the epoch of Charles V.

7 Gustave Reese, *Music in the Renaissance* (New York, 1954); Reinhard Strohm, *The Rise of European Music 1350–1550* (Oxford, 1993); as well as the works cited in note 17 to this introduction and note 115 to chapter 3.

8 A particularly significant example is the monumental *Storia di Napoli,* 10 vols. (Naples, 1967–74), in which the first reference to music concerns sixteenth-century "villanelle alla napoletana."

Perhaps the field that profits the most from the research that led to these three lectures (published here in greatly revised and expanded form) is music history, in absorbing the work done by historians in other disciplines. But I hope that the reconsideration of historical facts and figures from a musical perspective will allow them to be understood differently as well, in a more complete and realistic context ("the way it really was").[9]

All three of these studies share the castle as a common setting, the place where music was commissioned and performed. The castle served as the "theater" for the musical entertainment[10] of a specific, clearly defined audience, the lord and his court of castle inhabitants and regular guests: whether at Oramala or Calaone, where troubadours visited the Malaspina and Este courts, or Pavia of Visconti rule, or Castel Nuovo in Naples, where Pietrobono and Aurelio Brandolini both offered memorable performances.

Life in the castle followed a precise ritual. Over the course of each year there would be military campaigns in the summer and repose in the winter. Normal daily activities included hunting, games, music, and dance, while on holidays there were tournaments, banquets, musical performances, and balls, in honor of key court figures or illustrious guests. Music was thus an essential element in this well-organized, "well-mannered"[11] society. When literature and art would indulge this society's passion for self-portrayal, music was present in imaginary castles as well: such as that of the noblewoman in *Remède de Fortune,*[12] or of Pierbaldo with his jongleur Sollazzo;[13] or the frescoes with scenes of courtly life that decorated castle halls from Castelroncolo,[14] to Issogne,[15] to the Este residence at Belfiore described by Sabadino degli Arienti.[16]

9   The history of medieval music must provide "its own specific, original, active, innovative contribution to the definition, or hopefully the redefinition, of the various epochs, of the different contexts, indeed of the entire period" (F. Alberto Gallo, *Musica e storia tra Medioevo e Età moderna* [Bologna, 1986], p. 28). In other words: "Let us make our own Middle Ages" (Christopher Page, "A Reply to Margaret Bent," *Early Music* 22 [1994]: 127).

10   Paul Zumthor, *La Lettre et la voix de la "littérature" médiévale* (Paris, 1987), pp. 245–68.

11   Norbert Elias, *Über den Prozess der Zivilisation,* vol. 1, *Wandlungen des Verhaltens in den weltlichen Oberschichten des Abendlandes* (Basel, 1939; Frankfurt, 1969); Eng. trans. *The Civilizing Process,* trans. Edmund Jephcott, vol. 1, *The History of Manners* (New York, 1978).

12   *Oeuvres de Guillaume de Machaut,* ed. Ernest Hoepffner, vol. 2 (Paris, 1911), pp. 123–47.

13   Santorre Debenedetti, *Il "Sollazzo": Contributi alla storia della novella, della poesia musicale e del costume nel Trecento* (Turin, 1922), pp. 169–77.

14   Howard Mayer Brown, "Catalogus: A Corpus of Trecento Pictures with Musical Subject," *Imago musicae* 5 (1988): 204–6.

15   Emanuela Lagnier, *Iconografia musicale in Valle d'Aosta* (Rome, 1988), pp. 91–114.

16   Werner L. Gundesheimer, *Art and Life at the Court of Ercole I d'Este: The "De triumphis religionis" of Giovanni Sabadino degli Arienti* (Geneva, 1972), pp. 67–72.

Whether in the city or country, the castle favored and fostered the constant aggregation and interaction of all manner of musical activity, ranging from composition to performance, and the craft of each individual was esteemed without hierarchical distinction. Examples abound: such as that of the two vielle players at the court of Monferrato who provided a melody for the troubadour Raimbaut de Vaquieras (which brings to mind the two vielle players at the court of Burgundy, whose melodies were said to be better than those of Dufay and Binchois);[17] or that of the composer Jacopo da Bologna and the jongleur Dolcibene together at the Visconti court (though Filippo Villani identified them in different professions, among the *musici* and *histriones* respectively);[18] or that of the orator-improvisor Aurelio Brandolini, the instrumentalist Pietrobono (who also served as barber while at the Este castle in Ferrara, a popular custom that persisted throughout Italy until recently),[19] and the composer and theorist Johannes Tinctoris, all three working at the Aragon court in Naples.

Music in the castle meant above all that the musician living or performing there was entirely dependent upon the lord his host. This made for the perpetuation of a kind of cultural vassalage, with its requisite feudal tribute.[20] Johannes Tinctoris would therefore dedicate his work to Beatrice of Aragon just as Raimbaut de Vaquieras had dedicated his to Beatrice of Monferrato more than two centuries earlier. The relationship between master and musician could then be of any one of several quite different types. At one extreme there was the phenomenon (not found elsewhere in the fourteenth-century repertoire) of texts set contemporaneously by two musicians at the Visconti court (Piero and Giovanni on one occasion, Bartolino and Nicolò on another), each possibly contending for the master's favor; in those same years Jacopo and Giovanni competed at the court of Mastino della Scala, who urged them on with the

---

17 Jeanne Marix, *Histoire de la musique et des musiciens de la cour de Bourgogne sous le règne de Philippe le Bon (1420–1467)* (Strasbourg, 1939), pp. 107, 117–18.

18 Filippo Villani, *Liber de origine civitatis Florentiae et eiusdem famosis civibus*, ed. G. C. Galletti (Florence, 1847), pp. 34–36.

19 Information furnished by Roberto Leydi.

20 Marc Bloch, *La Société féodale* (Paris, 1940); English edition: *Feudal Society*, trans. L. A. Manyon (Chicago and London, 1961), pp. 145–279.

promise of gifts ("tyranno eos irritante muneribus").[21] At the opposite
extreme the musician could even attain social equality with his lord, as in
the example of Raimbaut de Vaquieras raised to knighthood by Bonifacio
of Monferrato; or there would be the acknowledgment of equal excellence, as between Pietrobono and Ferdinand of Aragon. In any case, the
course of musical activity at court depended entirely on the lord of the
castle—on the state of his political affairs, his financial resources, his particular personality and interests, his tastes and preferences. Thus disconti-
nuity rather than continuity was the rule. Once the dynastic glory of the
twelfth and thirteenth centuries had faded, two hundred years were to
pass before we find another musical composition dedicated to a Monferrato: *Illustrissimo marchese,* which Franchinus Gaffurius wrote for Guglielmo
VIII.[22] An equally long interval lay between the Provençal homages in
music that the transalpine Aimeric de Pegulhan dedicated to Beatrice and
Giovanna d'Este, and those in French that the transalpine Guillaume
Dufay dedicated to Nicolò III d'Este (*C'est bien raison*) and perhaps his son
Leonello (*Seigneur Leon*).[23]

For the inhabitants of the castle, music meant essentially singing a
poetic text—whether in consort with other voices or accompanied by one
or more instruments—or dancing to the sound of instruments. This bipartition of music was often reflected in literary eulogies to one's lord. There
was Thomas I of Savoy, for instance, who "dansoit et chantoit mieux que
nul aultre"[24] (danced and sang better than anyone else), and Leonello
d'Este, "ovans saltibus" (glorying in dancing), who sang and accompanied
himself on the *lyra*.[25] The same bipartition was represented in musical
illustrations: whether the scenes of accompanied singing and dancing in
the illuminations for the Visconti *Tacuinum sanitatis;* or the two musical
images for those born under the sign of the planet Venus (youths singing
a French chanson and a couple dancing to the sound of a harp) in the

---

21   Villani, *Liber,* p. 34.
22   Luigi Cremascoli, "Note storiche sulla vita di F. Gaffurio," in *Franchino Gaffurio* (Lodi,
1951), p. 56.
23   Lewis Lockwood, *Music in Renaissance Ferrara 1400–1505* (Oxford, 1984), pp. 36–40.
24   Giulio Bertoni, *I trovatori d'Italia* (Modena, 1915), p. 8 n. 3.
25   *Epistolario di Guarino Veronese,* ed. Remigio Sabbadini, vol. 2 (Venice, 1916), p. 151.

copy of *De sphaera* illuminated at the Sforza court;[26] or the two pieces of music that appear in the marquetry decorating the walls of the study in the castle of Urbino—*Bella gerit,* in honor of Federico da Montefeltro, and *J'ai prins amours,* which had been choreographed for a court spectacle.[27] It even found a kind of theoretical confirmation in the two contiguous musical dialogues in Petrarch's *De remediis,* or the pedagogical work *De ingenuis moribus et liberalibus studiis adolescentie* by Pierpaolo Vergerio, who permitted the young noble both "cantu fidibusque laxare animum" (to relax with song and stringed instruments) and "ad sonos saltare et muliebres ducere choreas" (to dance to music and to lead women's dances).

For each of these two types of musical activity in the castle there was a corresponding genre of technical treatise that itself had direct ties to court life. For poetry in music there were such works as the rhyming dictionary *Donatz proensals,* directly related to the activities of Uc de Saint-Circ and in any case traceable to the court of Alberico da Romano at Treviso; *Summa artis rithimici vulgaris dictaminis* written by Antonio da Tempo and translated into Italian by Gidino da Sommacampagna (both produced at the Della Scala court of Verona);[28] and the *Illuminator* by Giacomo Borbo, *maestro di canto* in the *cappella* of Alfonso of Aragon. Treatises on dance included the teachings of Domenico da Piacenza for the Sforzas, thereafter in a version by Antonio Cornazzano that was dedicated first to Ippolita Sforza and then to Sforza Secondo; and the treatise by Guglielmo Ebreo da Pesaro, dedicated to Galeazzo Sforza[29] and, in a second edition, to Federico da Montefeltro.

Music in the castle was a pleasurable experience for its listeners, a source of joy. There is striking evidence of this in Provençal song, with its veritable aesthetic based upon a delightful melody ("gai so"); in the portrayal of singing and dancing as manifestations of "Gaudium" in Petrarch's

---

26   Modena, Biblioteca Estense, MS a X 214, fols. 9v–10r; Pietro Puliatti, *Il "De sphaera" estense* (Bergamo, 1969).

27   Nicoletta Guidobaldi, *La musica di Federico: Immagini e suoni alla corte di Urbino* (Florence, 1995).

28   F. Alberto Gallo, "Dal Duecento al Quattrocento," in *Letteratura italiana,* ed. Alberto Asor Rosa, vol. 6 (Turin, 1986), pp. 250–53.

29   Guglielmo Ebreo da Pesaro, *De pratica seu arte tripudii: On the Practice or Art of Dancing,* edited, translated, and introduced by Barbara Sparti (Oxford, 1993).

De remediis; and even in this definition provided by the greatest representative of court poetry and music: "musique est une science / qui veut qu'on rit, on chant, on dence," (music is a science / that makes one laugh, sing, dance).[30] No wonder then that music was deemed most appropriate to represent the pleasantness of courtly life in the illuminations for Giangaleazzo Visconti's Book of Hours. Its capacity to provide physical pleasure, joy in listening, and solace from life's difficulties would long continue to elicit praise and respect, from the "laxare animum" (relaxation) of Vergerio and Guarino and Valturio, to the "delectatio auris et animi" (delight for the soul and ear) of Campano, to the "prope necessaria voluptas" (all but necessary pleasure) of Andrea Brenta. This conception of music was no doubt consolidated thanks particularly to the diffusion among courtly circles of Aristotle's *Politics,* which affirms (in book 8) the value of musical pleasure. The first Latin translation was completed at the papal court by William of Moerbecke, and Charles V of France also commissioned a translation in French by Nicholas Oresme; a later Latin translation by Leonardo Bruni, dedicated to Pope Eugenius IV, was requested by the king of Naples, Alfonso of Aragon, and Donato Acciaioli's commentary carried a dedication to Federico da Montefeltro, duke of Urbino. Aristotle, however, taught that music not only provided pleasure to the senses, but also made an essential contribution to man's moral and civic development. The influence of this Aristotelian observation consequently created a body of pedagogical literature that prescribed the teaching and exercise of music in the education of the prince, the noble, the man of court: from *De regimine principum* by Egidio Romano, dedicated to Philip the Fair of France; to Vergerio's *De ingenuis moribus et liberalibus studiis adolescentie,* dedicated to Ubertino da Carrara, son of Francesco I, lord of Padua; to *De liberorum educatione* by Enea Silvio Piccolomini, dedicated to Ladislaus of Hungary; to *De principe* by Giovanni Pontano, dedicated to Ferrante of Aragon; to *De eruditione principis* by Giovanni Garzoni, dedicated to Giovanni II Bentivoglio, lord of Bologna.

---

30 Guillaume de Machaut, *Poésies lyriques,* ed. Vladimir F. Chichmaref, vol. 1 (Paris, 1909), p. 10.

For medieval man, power was divided between two supreme authorities: the "Papatus" and the "Imperiatus," as Dante wrote, sometimes imagined as the "due magna luminaria" (two great bodies of light) regulating human life, the sun and the moon.[31] It therefore seems logical that medieval music would be similarly divided between the places where these two institutions operate, the church and the castle, and that each should possess its own organization for musical activity, its own musical genres, its own concept of music. While the church (secular clergy and religious orders) has been an established point of reference for everything concerning sacred music since the beginning of music historiography, the castle (its feudal system and court) still awaits recognition as the other point of reference.

This volume, moreover, intends to help establish the court as a continuous, unifying influence through a long period of secular music. It is therefore essential to address the anthropological nature (transcending different moments and places) of the phenomenon of court music, as has been done for the analogous and related phenomenon of court literature.[32] One primary benefit to be had from an anthropological perspective is that it permits such troublesome musicological problems as oral tradition and improvisation (sometimes also ambiguously called "unwritten tradition")—which are frequently encountered in court music (and in the present text) and have been heretofore addressed in only circumscribed fashion[33]—to enjoy a better, broader understanding, in that "what we call 'oral transmission' is what most human beings throughout history have known simply as 'music'—something to play or hear rather than something to write or read."[34] During this long period both music and

---

31   *Monarchia*, 3: 4, 11.

32   Reto R. Bezzola, *Les origines et la formation de la littérature courtoise en Occident (500–1200)*, vol. 3 (Geneva and Paris, 1984), pp. 524–39.

33   On the oral tradition of the troubadours, see Henrik van der Werf, *The Chansons of the Troubadours and Trouvères* (Utrecht, 1972); on the unwritten tradition of the Italian Quattrocento, see Nino Pirrotta, "Novelty and Renewal in Italy 1300–1600," in *Studien zur Tradition in der Musik: Kurt von Fischer zum 60. Geburtstag* (Munich, 1973), pp. 49–63; on improvisation, see James Haar, "*Improvvisatori* and Their Relationship to Sixteenth-Century Music," in *Essays on Italian Poetry and Music in the Renaissance, 1350–1600* (Berkeley, Los Angeles, and London, 1986), pp. 76–99.

34   Peter Jeffery, *Re-envisioning Past Musical Cultures: Ethnomusicology in the Study of Gregorian Chant* (Chicago, 1992), p. 124.

ideas about music changed along with the institution to which they were
tied. From the days when the court was primarily defined as "Armes,
amours, dames, chevalerie"[35] ("Le donne, i cavallier, l'arme, gli amori"
[damsels and knights, love and war], wrote Ariosto in evoking images of
that world),[36] music was there to brighten this life, as we read in the
descriptions of Raimbaut de Vaquieras and Immanuel Romano; and later,
when the court became a state government, promoting the establishment
of libraries and universities (Pavia, Ferrara, Naples), music would become
a significant part of this cultural world as well.

35   *Oeuvres complètes de Eustache Deschamps,* ed. Le Marquis de Queux de Saint-Hilaire, vol.
1 (Paris, 1878), p. 243.
36   *Orlando furioso,* 1: 1.

One

THE PROVENÇAUX
IN ITALY

En vostra cort renhon tug benestar:
dar e dompney, belh vestir, gent armar,
trompas e joc e viulas e chantar.[1]

In your court reign all proprieties:
munificence and homage to noblewomen, elegant dress, fine weapons,
trumpets and amusements and vielles and singing.

I

The above is a eulogy of court life in Monferrato at the dawn of the thirteenth century, taken from a letter Raimbaut de Vaquieras composed in
verse and addressed to his lord and companion, the marquis Bonifacio I.

This exemplification of court etiquette—that is, the court's characteristic code of values and comportment—reflects an expert, attentive hand
in the way the various items are ordered and combined. First and foremost is the lord's munificence; his generosity toward those who worked
with and for him, his inclination toward largesse, provided an indispensable economic foundation for the very existence of court life. Next to
munificence is homage to noblewomen, equally indispensable whether as
a social custom or, perhaps even more, as a practice elaborated in the cre-
ative arts. Then we find the image the court had of itself: elegant dress

---

1   *The Poems of the Troubadour Raimbaut de Vaquieras*, ed. Joseph Linskill (The Hague,
1964); music in *Las cançons del trobadors*, ed. Ismael Fernandez de la Cuesta (Toulouse, 1969),
pp. 321–33.

(the women) and fine weapons (the lord and knights)—or also the image that the court presented of itself: court festivities (elegant dress) and military campaigns (fine weapons). These images take on additional depth with the sound of trumpets (beyond the castle walls, as they accompany knights in battles and tournaments) and the pleasure of games (pastimes within the castle during periods of peace). Finally, instrumental music and poetry in song. The vielle is the instrument of court dances, of accompaniment for the troubadour or jongleur. Singing is the musical rendition of a poetic text, the moment and means of presenting a work composed (whether invented or assembled) by the poet-musician: the specific activity of the troubadour at court. Thus this eulogy of the perfect court situation opens with the virtue of the lord (the "dar" of Bonifacio), and closes, after an itineration through further examples, with the talent of his troubadour (the "chantar" of Raimbaut de Vaqueiras).

The court of Monferrato was the earliest point of contact for Provençal poets and musicians who migrated to Italy,[2] probably attracted by the political prestige and European fame that the Monferrato name enjoyed at the end of the twelfth century. It is perhaps telling that Peirol,[3] who would seem never to have been in Italy himself, was already singing around 1190 of

quel mar-ques va - lens __ e ____ pros __

that valiant and daring marquis

Corrado of Monferrato, at that time in the Holy Land for the Third Crusade. And Arnaut de Mareilh,[4] for whom we also lack any trace of residence in Italy, concluded one of his chansons:

2   Alessandro Barbero, "La corte dei marchesi di Monferrato allo specchio della poesia trobadorica," *Bollettino storico-bibliografico subalpino* 81 (1983): 641–703.

3   *Peirol, Troubadour of Auvergne,* ed. Stanley C. Aston (Cambridge, 1953); music in *Las cançons,* pp. 486–510.

4   *Les poésies lyriques du troubadour Arnaut de Maroill,* ed. Ronald C. Johnston (Paris, 1935); music in *Las cançons,* pp. 236–46.

mas quil mar - ques men-tan de Mon-fer - rat___

ja nol_ laus___ plus,_ c'as-satz l'a ben lau - dat_

but that marquis of Monferrato
I will praise no more, since I have already praised him enough.

This would have been in reference to Corrado's younger brother and successor, Bonifacio I. Such homages, first offered from afar, would later be rendered in person when Bonifacio decided to acquire that same ornament of poetry in music that had already been a long-established fixture in the most important courts of Europe.

One particularly significant figure was certainly the aforementioned Raimbaut de Vaquieras, who had visited the court of Monferrato on various occasions before establishing residence there in 1197. According to his *vida,* or biography, "cresc si de sen e d'armas e de trobar" (he rose [above others] in spirit, battle, and poetry).[5]

In fact, Raimbaut was not only a poet and musician for Bonifacio, but also his companion in combat: raised to knighthood, he would follow his lord when Bonifacio left Monferrato to lead the Fourth Crusade in 1202. As Raimbaut's biography states, he consequently received "gran terra e gran renda el regisme de Salonic. E lai el morì" (an important fief and handsome revenue in the kingdom of Thessalonica. And there he died).

Of the poetic texts Raimbaut dedicated to personages at the court of Monferrato, seven have come down to us with the melodies to which they were set. Four were written for Beatrice, daughter of Bonifacio I, and another mysterious woman addressed as "Bels Cavalliers"; they are *Eram requir son costum e son us, Savis e fol,* and two others that share an identical opening theme (reinforced by respective melodies that begin with the same notes) of war waged against love:

5   *Biographies des troubadours,* ed. Jean Boutière, Alexander H. Schutz, and Irénée M. Cluzel (Paris, 1973), pp. 447–48.

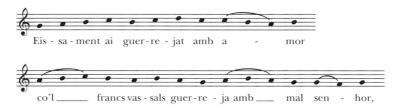

Eis - sa - ment ai guer-re - jat amb a   -   mor

co'l ____ francs vas - sals guer-re - ja amb ____ mal sen - hor,

I have warred against love exactly
as a proud vassal wars against an evil lord,

and

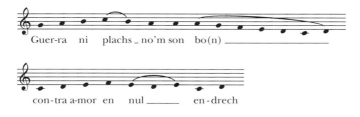

Guer-ra   ni   plachs _ no'm son   bo(n) _____

con-tra a-mor en   nul _____   en-drech

Neither wars nor treaties are useful to me
against love in any way.

Ara pot hom connoisser e provar, probably written around the time of the
departure for the Crusade in 1202, is dedicated to "Bels Cavalliers" alone
and "signed" by the author as both poet and musician:

Bels Ca - val - liers per cui   fatz _   sos _   et __   motz

Bels Cavalliers, for whom I write the melody and words.

Another text dedicated to "Bels Cavalliers," the descort[6] *Eras quam vey
verdeyar,* consists of five strophes each in a different language (Provençal,
Italian, French, Gascon, and Galician-Portuguese), followed by a sixth
strophe with each of its five lines similarly disposed. The musical setting,
which has not survived, would be particularly interesting because it apparently changed at every strophe as did the words and languages: "los motz
e·ls sos e·ls lenguatges" (the words, the melodies, and the languages).

---

6 DESCORT: a Provençal form akin to the *lai;* lyric poetry of irregular verse form. Many
have twelve stanzas (double strophes), each having formally identical halves, in a pattern that
varies from one verse to the next; the first and last stanzas are frequently related or identical
in form and music.

Non m'agrad'ivers ni pascor, written probably at Thessalonica in 1204–5, was dedicated to "Bels Cavalliers" and another personage given the fictitious name of "Engles" (Englishman), most likely the same Bonifacio of Monferrato. The two *senhals* (pseudonyms) are in the same position in two different strophes, so that they were therefore sung to the same music:

Pois mos Bels Ca - val - liers gra - zitz
Bells dous En - gles franc et ar - ditz

e jois m'es loi - gnatz _ e fu - gitz
cor - tes, es - se - nhatz, _ es - ser - nitz

Since my dear Bels Cavalliers
and joy have departed and fled from me . . .

Handsome, kind Engles, frank, bold,
courteous, learned, and astute . . .

One composition, *Calenda maia,* contains all three names—Beatrice, "Bels Cavalliers," and "Engles." A manuscript copied in Italy in the early fourteenth century[7] also provides the *razo,* or an account of the circumstances, whether real or imaginary, that inspired the work. There we read that Raimbaut had fallen into a state of deep melancholy and given up all poetic and musical activity after false accusations spread by malevolent courtiers caused him to be estranged from Beatrice.[8] However:

En aquest temps vengeron dos joglars de Franza en la cort del marqes, qe sabion ben violar. Et un jorn violaven una stampida que plazia fort al marqes et als cavaliers e a las dompnas.

At that time two jongleurs who were skillful players on the vielle came from France to the court of the marquis. And one day they played an estampida that greatly pleased the marquis, the knights, and the noblewomen.

Upon entreaty from Bonifacio and then Beatrice, Raimbaut recovered his spirits and took up poetry once again, writing the text of this chanson, *Calenda maia,* which "fu facta a las notas de la stampida que·l jo[g]lars fasion

---

7   Florence, Biblioteca Medicea Laurenziana, MS pluteo XLI, 42.

8   *Biographies des troubadours,* pp. 465–66.

en las violas" (was composed to the melody of the estampida that the jongleurs had played on the vielles).

The essential elements in this anecdote of court life are the same as
those in the passage from Raimbaut's letter in verse to Bonifacio, so that
the *razo* of *Calenda maia* almost seems to be its narrative version: the lord's
generosity, homage to the noblewoman, the sound of the vielle, and the
song of the troubadour.

The court of Monferrato was so famous in this period that Peire
Vidal,[9] who passed some time there writing a number of chansons, was
forced to observe ironically:

> *Tant an ben dig del marques*
> *joglar truant e garbier*
> *que tuit en so vertadier*
> *qu'ieu no sai que m'en disses.*

> So well have they spoken of the marquis,
> the jongleurs false and dishonest,
> who never tell the truth,
> that I no longer know what to say.

Vidal was by reputation an excellent musician, both as performer and
as composer. His biography states that "cantava meilz c'ome del mon" (he
sang better than anyone else in the world) and that "fo aquels que plus ric
sons fetz" (it was he who composed the most beautiful melodies).[10] Since
some sort of musical ability was a common characteristic (as we shall see)
of all the troubadours who came to Italy, it seems reasonable to assume
that this talent was particularly sought and esteemed by a society that itself
had no tradition of setting poetry to music.[11]

Vidal clearly considered the music for his chansons to be important,
often boasting that he was as skillful a musician as a poet:

9   Peire Vidal, *Poesie,* ed. D'Arco Silvio Avalle (Milan and Naples, 1960); music in *Las
cançons,* pp. 340–66.

10   *Biographies des troubadours,* pp. 351–52.

11   Aurelio Roncaglia, "Sul 'divorzio tra musica e poesia' nel Duecento italiano," *L'ars
nova italiana del Trecento* 4 (1978): 365–97.

Ajostar e lassar
sai tant gent motz e so

I know how to join and sunder
many beautiful texts and melodies

and

Per qu'ieu cobre chansos
gaias et ab gais sos.

Therefore I compose chansons
that are cheerful, with cheerful melodies.

Unfortunately, no melodic settings survive for any of the texts written during his stay at Monferrato.

Around 1190, Gaucelm Faidit, who was then still working in Provence and dedicating his chansons to Marie de Ventadorn, expressed his hope to pass through northern Italy on his way to the Holy Land:[12]

pas-sat a - ga la ___ mar part Lom-bar - di - a

I would have crossed the sea beyond Lombardy.

Gaucelm's biography makes a clear distinction between his scant performing ability and his competence as a poet and musician: "E cantava peiz d'ome del mon; e fetz molt bos sos e bos motz" (and he sang worse than any man on earth; and he composed many good melodies and good lyrics).[13]

Among the surviving chansons composed by Gaucelm at the court of Bonifacio of Monferrato after 1195, only *S'om pogues partir son voler* still possesses its melodic setting. It concludes thus:

chan - soss, _ vai ___ t'en _

12 *Les poèmes de Gaucelm Faidit*, ed. Jean Mouzat (Paris, 1965); music in *Las cançons*, pp. 268–311.

13 *Biographies des troubadours*, p. 167.

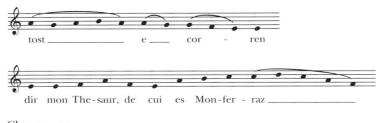

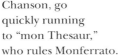

Chanson, go
quickly running
to "mon Thesaur,"
who rules Monferrato.

"Mon Thesaur" (my treasure) was the fictitious name Gaucelm used for Bonifacio, perhaps in clever allusion to the handsome gifts he received from the marquis. As his biography states: "E missers lo marques Bonifacis de Monferrat mes lo en aver et en rauba et en ten gran pretz lui e sas cansos" (and the lord marquis Bonifacio of Monferrato furnished him with riches and clothing and held him and his chansons in high regard).

Upon Bonifacio's death in distant battle in 1207, the rule of Monferrato passed to his son Guglielmo VI. Elias Cairel, who had been at Thessalonica (and thus in contact with Bonifacio), resided in Italy from 1210 to 1225, and dedicated several of his compositions to Guglielmo.[14] *Mout mi platz lo doutz temps d'abrils* closes with

> *Cansoneta, vait'en tost e viatz*
> *drech al marques de cui es Monferratz.*

> Chansonnette, go quickly and
> directly to the marquis who rules Monferrato.

It surely had a melodic setting as well, since the author declared himself to be the composer of its "gai motz ab so plazen" (cheerful words with pleasing melody).

Cairel certainly did not enjoy much respect, especially as a musician: "Mal cantava e mal trobava e mal violava e peichs parlava" (he sang poorly, wrote poetry poorly, played the vielle poorly, and spoke still worse), his biography records.[15] It adds, moreover, that "he carefully transcribed the

---

14   *Der Trobador Elias Cairel,* ed. Hilde Jaeschke (Berlin, 1921).
15   *Biographies des troubadours,* pp. 252–53.

texts and melodies"; but an ironic twist of fate would have it that not a single note of his music has survived.

The same destiny befell other settings for texts in honor of Guglielmo VI, written by troubadours who stopped at Monferrato but then moved on to spend the greater part of their careers at other Italian courts: Albertet de Sisteron, Guillem Augier Novella, and Aimeric de Pegulhan. Nonetheless, Guglielmo IV was not the last of the Monferrato dynasty to appear in Provençal song. When in 1280 Guglielmo VII accompanied his daughter Margherita to Castile for her marriage to King Alfonso, Guiraut Riquier[16] would celebrate the occasion thus:

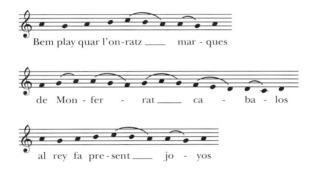

Bem play quar l'on-ratz ____ mar - ques
de Mon - fer - rat ____ ca - ba - los
al rey fa pre - sent ____ jo - yos

I am quite pleased that the honorable, illustrious
marquis of Monferrato
offers a joyful gift to the king.

II

With Bonifacio's departure for the Crusade and the consequent absence of patronage in Monferrato, Peire Vidal went on to pass the years 1204–6 at the court of the Genoese count Enrico Pescatore, lord of Malta:

A   Mau - ta,   ou   sui   al - ber - gatz

---

16 Guiraut Riquier, *Las cansos,* ed. Ulrich Mölk (Heidelberg, 1962); music in *Las cançons,* pp. 605–95.

ab   lo___   comt'_ En-ric de que'm_ platz

In Malta, where I have taken lodging
with count Enrico, whom I like.

In the conclusion of this composition the author declares himself "senher dels Genoes" (lord of the Genoese), and at the end of another chanson written in the same period he even claims to be "emperaire des Genoes" (emperor of the Genoese).

The activity of Folquet de Romans[17] in the beginning of the thirteenth century is more directly related to things Ligurian. His sirventes[18] *Far vuelh un nou sirventes,* written in 1220 and addressed to emperor Frederick II, mentions various Italian lords with whom the author may have stayed (Guglielmo VI of Monferrato, Azzo VI d'Este), and it concludes with an envoi[19] to Ottone del Carretto, lord of Savona:

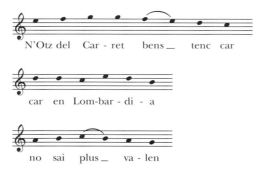

N'Otz del Car - ret   bens___   tenc car

car en Lom-bar - di - a

no sai plus___ va - len

Lord Ottone del Carretto, I hold you dear
because in Lombardy
I know no one more valiant.

But the most important center of poetic and musical activity was, after Monferrato, the court of the Malaspina dynasty, lords of Lunigiana, for whom the art of the troubadours was an established family tradition.

17   *L'oeuvre poétique de Folquet de Romans troubadour* (Aix, 1987); music in *Las cançons,* p. 542.

18   SIRVENTES (Provençal): a type of satirical troubadour poetry using strophic forms and concerning topical issues such as politics, literature, current events, the crusades, but not love.

19   ENVOI: a concluding half-stanza that usually begins with some form of address, such as "Prince." It repeats the refrain line and the rhyme scheme of the immediately preceding lines.

Raimbaut de Vaquieras was certainly in Liguria and at the Malaspina court during his second sojourn in Italy, between 1190 and 1195. Both his tenso[20] with a Genoese woman, which mentions Obizzino Malaspina, and another tenso with Alberto Malaspina, brother-in-law of Bonifacio of Monferrato, are from this period. Unfortunately, neither text has come down to us with its melody. A sirventes entitled *Honratz es bon per dependre*,[21] written for Alberto's son Moroello, was certainly set to music, since its anonymous author specified:

> *Serventes, tals sap ton son*
> *qui non enten ta razon.*
>
> Sirventes, there are those who know your melody
> but do not understand your story.

The earliest surviving music therefore dates from the epoch of Moroello's sons, Guglielmo and Corrado, particularly the decade 1210–20.

Another troubadour at the Malaspina court, Peire Raimon, had previously been at the court of Alfonso II of Aragon, where he passed the last years of the twelfth century.[22] His only surviving musical composition can be traced to that period. The text, which begins with a comparison (like many others by this poet),[23] is a love lament but also a reflection on the condition of the poet-musician:

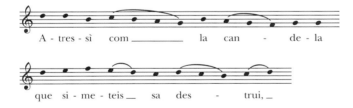

A - tres - sì com _____ la can - de - la
que si - me - teis __ sa des - trui, __

---

20   TENSO (Provençal): a form of troubadour poetry consisting of a discussion in dialogue form between two or more poets maintaining opposing views on a given topic, usually love.

21   *Poesie provenzali storiche relative all'Italia*, ed. Vincenzo De Bartholomaeis, vol. 1 (Rome, 1931), pp. 68–70.

22   *Le poesie di Peire Raimon de Tolosa*, ed. Alfredo Cavaliere (Florence, 1935); music in *Las cançons*, pp. 376–78.

23   Martin de Riquer, *Los trobadores: Historia literaris y textos*, vol. 2 (Barcelona, 1975), pp. 933–34.

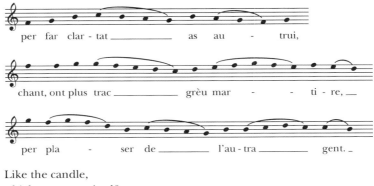

per far clar - tat ⸻ as au - trui,

chant, ont plus trac ⸻ grèu mar - - ti - re, ⸻

per pla - ser de ⸻ l'au - tra ⸻ gent. ⸺

Like the candle,
which consumes itself
to provide light for others,
I sing, suffering the depths of martyrdom
for the pleasure of others.

Raimon's biography highlights his human virtues and his ability as poet and performer: "El era saus hom e suptils e saub ben trobar e cantar" (he was wise, kind, and subtle, and he was a good poet and singer).[24]

At least one of the poems he dedicated to Guglielmo Malaspina, *Pus vey parer la flor el glay,* was undoubtedly set to melody, in light of the explicit references within the text itself:

> *De far chanso m'espres talans*
> *ab motz plazens et ab so guay;*
> *e pus de ben amar melhur,*
> *segon razo,*
> *trop en dey far mielhs motz e so.*
>
> I wish to write a chanson
> with pleasing words and with a cheerful melody;
> and since loving well improves me,
> as is just,
> I will certainly write much better words and melody.

Other frequent references to melodic settings in his texts are extremely helpful in understanding the function ascribed to the music as these works were conceived. Indeed, from the beginning of one text it would appear that the music was an element of primary importance:

---

24 *Biographies des troubadours,* p. 347.

Ab son gai, plan e car
faz descort leu e bon,
avinen per chantar
e de bella razon.

With a cheerful melody, easy and praiseworthy,
I fashion a descort light and good,
pleasant to sing
and with a beautiful subject.

The melodic setting is portrayed here in terms of three different characteristics: cheerful, producing joy in the listener; easy, lacking any difficulty (for both performer and listener); and at the same time praiseworthy, of high stylistic quality. The definition of the poetic text (the descort) seems to follow the same pattern, since the text is meant to be sung ("per chantar") and not simply read. Thus "leu" and "bon" would correspond to "plan" and "car," while the beauty of the subject ("bella razon") at the end of the strophe can be read in conjunction with the cheerfulness of the music ("gai son") at the beginning. This appraisal of text and music independently of one another was perhaps more than just a theoretical analysis: it seems possible that in performance they were presented separately first, then combined. At the end of one composition, Peire Raimon specified the following:

E vuel qe l'apregna
cobletas, viulan
e pois en chantan.

And I want you to hear
the short strophes, played on the vielle
and then sung.

If this intention is taken literally, one can suppose that the performer first recited the poetic text, then played the melody alone on his instrument (thus allowing the listener to appreciate each one as a distinct and equally important element), and finally united them in song.

Confirmation of such a procedure can apparently be had from the text of another Provençal troubadour who was present at the Malaspina court, Albertet de Sisteron.[25] In concluding one of his chansons he turns to the performer with the following enjoinder:

---

25   Jean Boutière, ed., "Les poésies du troubadour Albertet," *Studi medievali* 16 (1937): 1–129; music in *Las cançons,* pp. 518–22.

Peirol, violatz e chantatz cointamen
de ma chanzon los motz e·l son leugier.

Peirol, play the vielle and gracefully sing
the words and lightsome melody of my song.

Coming at the end of the recited text, this prescription would serve to introduce the music to follow.

According to his biography, Albertet was actually more respected as musician than as poet: "fez assatz de cansos, que aguen bon sons e motz de pauca valenza" (he wrote many chansons that had good melodies and words of little worth); at court he was in particular demand "per lo bons sons qu'el fasia" (for the good melodies that he wrote).[26]

This unusually high regard for Albertet's musical gifts would seem to be confirmed by his apparent wealth of melodic invention: in fact, there is virtually no repetition of melodic material in any of his three surviving settings, contrary to common practice. One minor exception occurs in *Mon coratges s'es cambiats*, where the music for the first line is repeated (though varied at the beginning) for the third line. In *En mon cor ai tal amor enconbida*, the repetition of "Amors" at the beginning of the fifth line of each of the first three strophes makes for a curiously persistent association of the word with the musical motive:

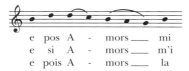

In the second strophe of *A mi non fai chantar folia ni flors,* the relationship between poet-musician and lord is described in terms of a reciprocal give and take:

sui __ eu, qi   mais __ non voil chan-tar ail-lors

I am like one who changes lords many times
until he finds one who does him great honor;
I no longer wish to sing for others.

It was understood that the lord would manifest his appreciation in concrete terms to the troubadour for his work; in return, the troubadour would go forth singing praises of the lord and his consort to others:

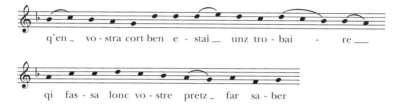

q'en __   vo - stra cort ben e - stai __ unz tro - bai   -   re __

qi   fas - sa lonc vo - stre   pretz __ far   sa - ber

since in your court there is certainly room for a troubadour
who makes your merits known in distant places.

There are references to music at the beginnings of three chansons by Albertet; evidently these chansons originally possessed melodic settings that have since disappeared. The practice of beginning a piece of poetry with a declaration of one's literary poetics was frequent among the troubadours and the trouvères as well;[27] but Albertet, since he was also a good musician, chose instead to emphasize the presence and function of the melodic setting. In his case it seems that the musical element (the composer of the melody, the composed melody) was already present (both in essence and in physical fact) when the text was written. It is significant that these observations always occur in the first strophe, since they function as a sort of explanatory introduction for the audience, almost an *accessus* into the work itself. One of Albertet's chansons all but literally repeats the previously cited passage by Peire Raimon, analyzing the constituent elements of the work in a progression from the cheerfulness of the externally perceptible sound to joy as motivation from within:

27 Marcello Venturi, "Ancora un caso di intertestualità fra trovieri e trovatori," *Medioevo romanzo* 13 (1988): 321–29.

Ab son gai e leugier
vuoill far gaia chansso,
car de gaia razo
son miei gai cossirier
que m'ant dich q'ieu retraia
chansson coindeta e gaia.

With a cheerful and lightsome melody
I wish to write a cheerful chanson,
because I have a cheerful subject matter
for my cheerful thoughts,
which have told me to compose
a graceful and cheerful chanson.

In another instance he pursues the opposite path, moving from inner joy
to the cheerful, externally perceptible melody:

Ab joi comensi ma chanson
qu'en joi es mos cors e mos sens,
que·l jois d'amor, c'autres jois vens,
me prega e·m ditz e·m somon
qu'eu chant; et ai ben rason,
pois d'amor es mos cossiriers,
qu'eu fassa gais sons e leugiers.

With joy I begin my chanson,
since my heart and my senses are immersed in joy,
since the joy of love, which surpasses any other joy,
beseeches me, tells me, entreats me
to sing; and I have good reason,
since my thoughts are of love,
to create cheerful and lightsome melodies.

Still another chanson begins similarly but more concisely:

Pos en ben amar m'esmer,
a far m'er
gaia chanzon
ab gai son
e leu.

Because I purify myself in true love,
I must create
a cheerful chanson
with a melody cheerful
and light.

"Gai" and "leu," the two constant attributes of "so," evidently constitute a summary formula of Albertet's musical poetics—one that was shared, as we have seen and shall see, by other troubadours working in Italy. "Leu" seems to possess more technical connotations, given that it is clearly a principle of literary poetics, the "trobar leu,"[28] transferred here to a musical context; it must mean that the composer intended to create music that could be easily managed by any type of player or public. "Gai" has, on the other hand, a more general significance, since in the texts of Albertet and other troubadours it refers not only to the melody, but also to the poetic text, the reason for that text, and the mood of the author.[29] "Gai" also describes the woman beloved, service in the name of love—and indeed, life itself at court. The "gai so," the cheerful melody, is therefore music that is part and parcel of a comprehensive view of life, rendering it complete.

Albertet exchanged verses with Aimeric de Pegulhan, another Provençal troubadour in Italy. The resulting tenso they created was based on a question of love: whether, between two women of equal merit, it is better to choose the woman one loves more but without hope of return, or the woman loved less but reciprocally. Aimeric, who favored the second solution, designated Beatrice d'Este as his referee (it was to her, as we shall see, that he addressed his musical homages), while Albertet, who favored the first, indicated as referee Emilia di Romagna. Emilia, of the noble Guidi family of Ravenna, was wed in 1216 to Pietro Traversari, a marriage arranged to restore peaceful relations between the two families. It is possible that Albertet also spent some time in Romagna, and perhaps he was not the only Provençal troubadour to do so. In fact, there is a descort written for Emilia by Guillem Augier Novella,[30] who had passed through the Monferrato and Malaspina courts. His biography states: "Estet lonc temps en Lombardia. E fez de bons descortz."[31] (He spent much time in Lombardy. And he wrote good descorts.) In the tenth strophe of one of these descorts, *Ses alegrage*, we read:

28   Ulrich Mölk, *Trobar clus Trobar leu: Studien zur Dichtungslehre der Trobadors* (Munich, 1968).

29   Glynnis M. Cropp, *Le vocabulaire courtois de troubadours de l'époque classique* (Geneva, 1975).

30   *Il trovatore Guillem Augier Novella*, ed. Monica Calzolari (Modena, 1986); music in *Las cançons*, p. 531.

31   *Biographies des troubadours*, p. 488.

She merits well
(whoever would object),
my lady Emilia in Romagna,
the great worth
with which she infuses
her body, cheerful, pleasing,
and gentle.

III

The center of activity for early thirteenth-century Provençal troubadours
in the Veneto region was the court of marquis Azzo VI d'Este.[32] Aimeric
de Pegulhan had been in his service for some time, and when the marquis

---

32   Gianfranco Folena, "Tradizione e cultura trobadorica nelle corti e nelle città venete,"
in *Culture e lingue nel Veneto medievale* (Padua, 1990), pp. 1–137.

died in 1212 the poet wrote two funeral laments.[33] In the second one he expressed his ironic concern for the fate of the numerous jongleurs at the Este court who were now left without a patron:

> *que faran li joglar,*
> *a cui fesetz tant dos,*
> *tant honors?*
> *Mas un conselh no·n sai al trobadors:*
> *laisso·s morir ez anous lai sercar.*

> what will become of the jongleurs,
> to whom you made so many gifts,
> so many favors?
> I have but one suggestion to give the troubadours:
> that they die and seek you thither.

The first to succeed, briefly, to Azzo's reign was his elder son Aldobrandino, after which the title passed in 1215 to Azzo's much younger son Azzo VII. Aimeric spent the last years of his life at this court, as his biography states: "Puois s'en venc en Lombardia, on tuich li bon ome li feron gran honor. Et en Lombardia definet."[34] (He then went to Lombardy, where the gentlemen all did him great honor. And in Lombardy he died.) The opinion of his performing ability was anything but positive: "Apres cansos e sirventes, mas molt mal cantava" (he knew chansons and sirventes, but he sang very poorly). Yet his efforts as composer were hardly consigned to oblivion, since no fewer than five of his poems written at the Este court have come down to us with their music.

One text that Aimeric sent to Sordello,[35] the most famous of the Italian troubadours who was then at the court of Treviso, begins with what is perhaps an ironic allusion to the non-musical, purely literary tradition of Italian poetry:

> *Can qu·m fezes vers ni cançe*
> *eras voil far moz senes so.*

> Though I have written both verses and chansons,
> now I wish to write words without melody.

---

33 *The Poems of Aimeric de Pegulhan*, ed. William P. Shepard and Frank M. Chambers (Evanston, 1950); music in *Las cançons*, pp. 391–402.

34 *Biographies des troubadours*, pp. 425–26.

35 Sordello, *Le poesie*, ed. Marco Boni (Bologna, 1954).

Actually, Sordello occasionally mentions a "gay so" or "leugier so" in his texts, but with reference to compositions written during his sojourn in Provence at the court of Raymond Berengar IV. His was therefore the opposite situation of an ultramontane troubadour, one trying to adjust to a context where it was common practice to set poetry to music. Little effort was necessary: it was sufficient to write a text with the same metric structure as one already set to music, and simply adopt that music for one's own purposes. This is perhaps what happened for the partimen[36] Sordello wrote with a fellow troubadour at the court of Provence, Bertran d'Alamanon, entitled *Bertrans, lo joy de dompnas e d'amia*. Sordello named Guida di Rodez as his referee while Bertran indicated Jean de Valery, and it was therefore resolved that the composition be sent "en Franza." Since this piece possesses the same metric structure as the chanson *S'onques nus hom pour dure departie* by the trouvère Hugues de Bercé, it would not be at all incongruous if the melody of this French source were also used for the occasion.[37]

Among the compositions Aimeric de Pegulhan wrote at the Este court is a collection dedicated to Beatrice, sister of Azzo VII, and to Guglielmo Malaspina. One piece from this group opens with a description of the court as the place where questions of poetic-musical form were debated:

Mangtas vetz sui enqueritz
en cort cossi vers no fatz;
per qu'ieu vuelh si' appellatz—
e sia lur lo chausitz—
chansos o vers aquest chans.
E respon als demandans
qu'om non troba ni sap devezio
mas sol lo nom entre vers e chanso.

Many times I have been asked
at court why I do not compose verses;
therefore I desire that this song be called—
and may the choice be theirs—
chanson or verse.

---

36   PARTIMEN (Provençal): a troubadour poetic genre in dialogue form, debating a question of love or some other subject, often with a judgment at the end from the lord or lady of the court; called "jeu-parti" in French.
37   The music is in Enrico Paganuzzi, "Medioevo e Rinascimento," in *La musica a Verona* (Verona, 1976), pp. 27–28.

And to those who ask, I respond
that one cannot detect nor understand any difference
other than in the name between verse and chanson.

If the "vers" and the "chanso" cannot be distinguished from one another
on the basis of the metric structure of the text, neither can they be distinguished by their melodic settings:[38]

e cortz sonetz e cochans
ai auzitz en verses mans,
ez auzida chansonet' ab lonc so,
e·ls motz d'amdos d'un gran e·l chant d'un to.

and melodies short and concise
I have heard with lengthy verses,
and I have heard brief chansons with long melodies,
and the words of both in like style and their song in like manner.

The musical setting for this composition is expressly mentioned in the
text, which is addressed in this case to Guglielmo Malaspina:

qu'elh aprenda de te los motz e·l so.

that he may hear your words and your melody.

Unfortunately that setting has not survived, but three other melodies for
texts in this collection fared better: *Atressim pren quom fai al jogador, En
Amor trob alques en qe·m refraing,* and *Per solatz d'autrui chant soven* are complete with their music.

Because he was well aware that his dedicatees and their courts were
knowledgeable about questions of style and the relationship between
poetry and music, Aimeric devoted his utmost to both elements in these
works. This seems especially evident in the last piece, where the troubadour meditates upon his art as a service that provides pleasure for others:

Per solatz d'autrui chant soven;
mas pero cora que chantes,
ni per bon respieich m'alegres,
ara vei que chant per nien.

---

38   Alfred Jeanroy, *La poésie lyrique des troubadours,* vol. 2 (Toulouse and Paris, 1934), pp.
64–67.

E sui a mon dan chantaire,
si cum l'auzels de bon aire,
que sap q'es pres e per so no is recre
c'ades non chant: atretal es de me.

I often sing for the pleasure of others;
but I have always sung
or rejoiced for good reason;
now, instead, I see that I sing in vain.
And I sing to my detriment,
like the gentle bird
who knows he has been captured and yet
does not stop singing: thus it has befallen me.

The most striking characteristic of this text is the systematic use of rhetorical devices based on the repetition of verbal sonorities, procedures that were theorized for Latin poetry[39] but also used by the troubadours. Here "chant," "chantes," and "chantaire" are the dominant theme and sound of the strophe, likening the image of the poet with that of the imprisoned bird. This procedure is attenuated in successive strophes, but it returns in an almost obsessive manner in the last strophe, this time on the verbal sonority of "merce," "merceies," "merceian," and "merceiaire" (note the identical positions of "merceiaire" and "chantaire" in their respective strophes), as the poetry closes in an anguished lament of love:

Dompna, per merce solamen
soffrissetz c'un pauc merceies
merces, e c'un pauc afranques
merceian vostre dur talen
vas mi, qe us sui merceiaire
totz temps e merce clamaire;
e merceians sui e serai jasse
vostr'om, clamans: "merce, merce, merce!"

My lady, for the sake of mercy alone,
pity me by being a bit merciful,
and by softening a bit,
with mercy, your hard heart
toward me, which I beseech
constantly and beg for mercy;
and in asking mercy, I am and will always be
your servant, crying: "mercy, mercy, mercy!"

---

39   Edmond Faral, *Les arts poétiques du XIIe et du XIIIe siècle* (Paris, 1924).

The melody of this chanson uses nothing more than the repetition of brief step-wise series of ascending and then descending notes, within the range of a third, fourth, or fifth, for every line of the strophe (only in the fourth line is the pattern reversed):

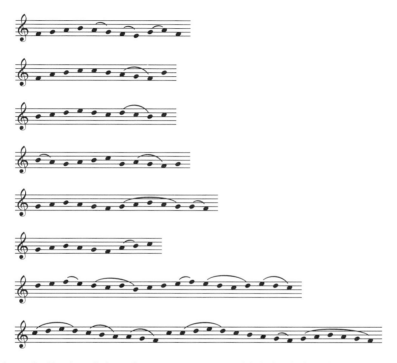

Such melodic simplicity, almost monotony, which is obviously the same for every strophe, may have been adopted precisely in order to avoid distracting the listener's attention from the verbal sonorities. These instead are carefully varied with each strophe: in addition to the series in the first and last strophes mentioned above, another series on "Amor," "ames," and "amaire" appears in the second strophe. This would seem to create a minimal, non-interferential rapport between poetry and music. On the other hand, however, the peculiar movement of the melodic line reflects a well-known procedure in musical rhetoric.[40] One could therefore hypothesize a system of analogies between the musical and verbal structures. The rise and fall of the melodic line would then perhaps correspond to the

40   F. Alberto Gallo, *La polifonia nel Medioevo* (Turin, 1991), pp. 10–11; English edition, *Music of the Middle Ages II* (Cambridge, 1985), pp. 7–8.

frequent positive-negative verbal juxtapositions, such as "desamatz amaire" (lover unloved) or "ses emperi emperaire" (emperor without an empire), both placed in the same position (close of the sixth line in the second and third strophes). Or it might correspond to certain retrograde procedures, such as "pe*ro* c*ora*" in line 2, "*am ma*is" in line 19, the even more obvious "c'un pauc merceies / merces, e c'un pauc" in lines 34–35, or "pr*os* Guillems Malaspina *so*stes" in line 41, thus enframing the name of one of the two dedicatees. If this system further implies a correlation between the musical structure and the theme of the chanson, then the incessant rise and fall of the melody, a series of fragments that always begin and end on the same note, could seem the most appropriate realization of the "chant per nien" of the poet and the "chant" of the captive bird.

Aimeric dedicated one of his compositions to Beatrice d'Este alone:

Anyone who sees her says of her:
because God has given so many
fine qualities to Lady Beatrice,
there is no escaping her charm.

Another, *Cel qui s'irais ni guerreia ab Amor,* seems to refer (at least according to the text furnished by one of the manuscripts) to Giovanna d'Este, wife of Azzo VII:

Na Zo - a - na d'Est, [ieu] dir no sa - bri - a

tant de leau-zor ____ com a _____ vos _ con-ven-ri - a

Lady Giovanna d'Este, [I] would not know how to express
as much praise as you would deserve.

In time, the Este family would leave the Veneto region to make Ferrara their seat of political power and artistic patronage.[41]

Giovanna d'Este was also the recipient of verses written by Uc de Saint-Circ,[42] a Provençal troubadour who spent most of his career at the court of Alberico da Romano in Treviso (himself a poet who wrote in Provençal and exchanged verses with Uc). The son of a minor feudal lord, Uc had been sent to Montpellier for university studies that he eventually abandoned. His biography praises him both as poet and as musician: "Cansos fez de fort bonas e de bos sons" (he composed chansons that were very good, with good melodies).[43]

By the time Uc arrived in Italy he already possessed considerable poetic and musical experience, which he had developed at various courts in southern France and Spain. Two compositions dedicated to Savaric de Monleon, *Anc enemics qu'ieu agués* and *Tres enemics e dos mals senhors ai,* and one dedicated to the countess of Provence, *Nuls om non sap d'amic, tro l'a perdut* (therefore written prior to his Italian period), are all that remain of his musical production. The first two belong to a group of four texts with the same opening theme: the poet's enemies, namely, his eyes and his heart. One begins:

Anc e - ne - mics _ qu'ieu a - gués

---

41   Lewis Lockwood, *Music in Renaissance Ferrara 1400–1505* (Oxford, 1984), pp. 9–10.

42   *Poésies de Uc de Saint-Circ,* ed. Alfred Jeanroy and Jean-Jacques Salverda de Grave (Toulouse, 1913); music in *Las cançons,* pp. 574–78.

43   *Biographies des troubadours,* pp. 239–40.

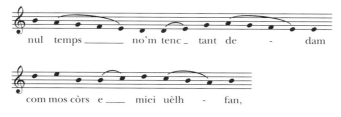

nul temps _____ no'm tenc _ tant de - dam

com mos còrs e ___ miei uèlh - fan,

Never an enemy that I have had
has done me greater harm than
now my eyes and my heart.

The other begins much the same:

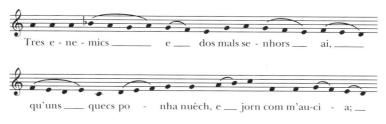

Tres e - ne - mics _____ e ___ dos mals se - nhors ___ ai, _____

qu'uns ___ quecs po - nha nuèch, e ___ jorn com m'au-ci - a; ___

I have three enemies and two evil lords,
each of which night and day tries to kill me.

During his sojourn in Treviso (circa 1226–50), Uc's musical inspiration
seems to have waned. It was not that his verses went without music in this
period, but rather that in certain cases, at least, he apparently preferred to
use melodies composed by others—perhaps in deference to Italian custom
(and possibly even Sicilian to some extent).[44] In a sirventes written around
1226 (addressed to the jongleur Messonget and including mention of both
Alberico da Romano and Azzo VII d'Este) Uc says explicitly:

> *El son d'En Arnaut Plagues.*
>
> The melody is by Master Arnaut Plagues.

Specifically, this melody originally accompanied the chanson *Ben volgra
midous sauber,* which Arnaut Plagues had written for Alfonso VIII of Castile,
and which possesses the same metric structure and the same rhyme
scheme. The music was used by others as well, but in spite of this fact it is

---

44 Joachim Schulze, *Sizilianische Kontrafakturen: Versuch zur Frage der Einheit von Musik
und Dichtung in sizilianischen und sikulo-toskanischen Lyrik des 13. Jahrhunderts* (Tübingen, 1989).

now lost to history.[45] Another sirventes that Uc wrote around 1240–41, during the siege of Faenza by Frederick II, begins:

> *Un sirventes vuelh far en aquest son d'en Gui.*

> I wish to write a sirventes on this melody by Master Gui.

This time the reference is to a melody previously used by poets named Gui (Gui de Nanteuil, Gui de Cavaillon), also lost even though it had remained popular up through the beginning of the fourteenth century.[46]

The last datable composition by Uc de Saint-Circ is again a sirventes, a harsh attack on Manfredi II Lancia (podestà of Milan in 1253), which is perhaps more a reflection of Alberico da Romano's hostility than his own. Its metric model was the sirventes *Casutz sui de mal en pena* by Bertran de Born, so we may therefore hypothesize that the melody[47] of this model—which in turn came from the chanson *Bele, douce dame chere* by the trouvère Conon de Béthune—was adopted as well:

Such poor company
and so wretched a figure is
that Manfredi
Lancia, whom they call marquis.

45 Friedrich Gennrich, *Die Kontrafakturen im Liedschaffen des Mittelalters* (Langen bei Frankfurt, 1965), pp. 11–12.
46 Roncaglia, "Sul 'divorzio tra musica e poesia,'" pp. 377–78.
47 The music is in *Las cançons*, p. 256.

Sirventes dealing with political issues (by no means a minor genre in troubadour poetry, including that of Italy) may in fact have been quite likely to
use melodies the public already knew and enjoyed, in order to stimulate a
greater diffusion of the text.

Several compositions by Uc de Saint-Circ begin with a declaration of
his poetics for both the text and the music. In one case he aspires to imitate his source of inspiration:

> *Aissi cum es coinda e gaia*
> *e cortesa e plazens*
> *ed azaut' a totas gens*
> *la bella de cui eu chan,*
> *m'es ops que d'aital semblan*
> *cum ill es fassa canso,*
> *coinda e gaia ab plazen so.*

> Just as she is charming and cheerful
> and courteous and pleasing
> and welcome with everyone,
> the beautiful woman of whom I sing,
> it is fitting that in complete likeness
> of her I write a chanson
> charming and cheerful, with pleasing melody.

Both text and music take part in this interplay of affinities: the first two
qualities of the woman, "charming" and "cheerful," correspond to those
of the "canso" (text), while a third quality, "pleasing," also describes the
"so" (music). Another chanson opens with a still more complete and precise theoretical statement, especially regarding its performance:

> *Chanzos q'es leus per entendre*
> *et avinenz per chantar,*
> *tal qu'om non puescha reprendre*
> *los motz ni·l chant esmendar,*
> *et a douz e gai lo son*
> *e es de bella razon*
> *ed avinen per condar,*
> *mi plai e la voil lauzar*
> *a qi la blasm' e defendre.*

> A chanson that is easy to understand
> and pleasant when sung,
> one that cannot be faulted

for the words, nor the song corrected,
and that has a sweet and cheerful melody,
and a fine subject,
and is pleasant to repeat,
is appealing to me, and I wish to praise it
and defend it against those who censure it.

This seeming conglomeration of elements is actually organized in a clear and logical sequence. If the text is easily understood by the audience and gives them pleasure when sung, no one will criticize either the words or the music. Toward this end it is indispensable both that the text develop a fine subject, and that the performance make use of a sweet and cheerful melody. Under these circumstances it is pleasant to listen to the work and also to hear it again. Uc seems to have been thinking not only of immediate production and reception, but also of the possibility that the text and music might be performed in times and contexts perhaps quite distant and different from those in which the work was created.[48]

How logical, therefore, that it would be Uc himself to assemble the first Italian collection of texts (and music?) of Provençal poetry, in a *Liber* for Alberico da Romano. He also had a major hand in editing the prose pieces, *Vidas* and *Razos,* that provide so much information (of a musical nature as well) on all the troubadours, including those who worked in Italy. Thanks to his initiatives, any performer had all the material necessary to present any piece in the repertory, and the audience of any court could avail itself of a kind of "concert program." For each author there was first a biography, then an explanation of what inspired the composition, and then the text (and music) of same. Often miniatures were also supplied as "portraits" of the poet-musicians.[49]

All this presupposed that performers and public alike were able to understand and appreciate the Provençal language (and music). We might therefore imagine that Uc de Saint-Circ was also the author of the *Donatz proensals,*[50] a grammar and rhyming dictionary of Provençal with

---

48   Maria Luisa Meneghetti, *Il pubblico dei trovatori: Ricezione e riuso dei testi lirici cortesi fino al XIV secolo* (Modena, 1984).

49   Ibid., pp. 325–63.

50   *The "Donatz Proensals" of Uc Faidit,* ed. John Henry Marshall (London, New York, and Toronto, 1969), pp. 112–13.

Latin translation, which was intended to help spread the knowledge of this language and poetry from beyond the Alps. The manual can in any case be traced to Treviso, since it was dedicated to Corrado da Sterleto, imperial podestà in Treviso at various times between 1234 and 1239. It includes not only technical musical terms in Provençal with their Latin equivalent,[51] but also lists of related words that pertain to some feature of musical life at court; for example, the following imperative verbs:

chanta	canta
bala	salta
vuila	viella
dance	ducat coream
saute	saltet
tombe	[cadet] vel ludat saltando

The second half of the thirteenth century saw more than these efforts at conservation, however, since we also have evidence of Provençal poetic and musical activity going on at that time in the eastern area of the Veneto region. In 1269 the death of the patriarch of Aquileia, Gregorio da Monte-longo, was commemorated by an anonymous author with a lengthy lament in Provençal; the text alone survives in a single Venetian music manuscript (which will be discussed later), along with its Latin transla-tion[52] (just like the *Donatz proensals*). The music for this composition is lost; but the melody (and only the first strophe of text) of another funeral lament, written in 1272 for Giovanni di Cucagna (a feudal lord in Friuli who was in contact with the rulers of Este and Treviso),[53] has survived. *Quar nueg e jorn trist soi et esbahit* praises the virtues of the deceased lord and sympathizes with his subjects for their tremendous loss:

---

51   Elizabeth Aubrey, "References to Music in Old Occitanian Literature," *Acta musicolog-ica* 61 (1989): 129 n. 66.

52   Paul Meyer, "Complainte provençale et complainte latine sur la mort du patriarche d'Aquilée Grégoire de Montemagno," in *In memoria di Napoleone Caix e Ugo Angelo Canello: Miscellanea di filologia e linguistica* (Florence, 1886), pp. 231–36.

53   Maurizio Grattoni, "Cavalieri erranti, menestrelli e tradizione musicale medioevale," in *Castelli del Friuli,* ed. Tito Miotti, vol. 4 (Udine, 1980), pp. 276–82.

cilh de Cu - canh plus non au - ran la lutz, _____

those of Cucagna will have their light no longer.

This anonymous author could have been either one of the last ultramontane poet-musicians come to work in the courts of northern Italy, or an Italian who had adopted practices learned from them.

From the mid-thirteenth to the mid-fourteenth century, the Veneto region became the principal center where texts of Provençal poetry were collected and copied; two-thirds of all known sources come from this period and region. In addition, of the only two manuscripts known in Provençal that also include musical settings, one comes from the Veneto.[54] It contains eighty-one melodies arranged by author, half of them unique, the remainder present in other music sources but with numerous and significant variations. Thus this particular codex may trace its textual tradition to a collection originating in southern France, but its musical tradition represents a repertory of melodies as they were known in northern Italy. The first thirteen melodies (two of them unique to this collection) are by Folquet de Marseille, the troubadour admired by Dante; two melodies by another "Dantesque" troubadour, Arnaut Daniel, are the only ones he is known to have written. As for troubadours who had come to work in Italy, there are eleven melodies (three of them unique) of the fourteen known to be by Gaucelm Faidit, the single known melody by Peire Raimon, five melodies (four of them unique) of the six known to be by Aimeric de Pegulhan, and the only three melodies known to be by Uc de Saint-Circ.

This same collection also contains the text of a short didactic poem attributed to Garin lo Brun, who lived around the middle of the twelfth century.[55] It must have been particularly well received in northern Italy, since another manuscript from the Veneto region is our only other

---

54 Milan, Biblioteca Ambrosiana, R 71 sup.; Agostino Ziino, "Caratteri e significato della tradizione musicale trobadorica," in *Lyrique romane médiévale: La tradition des chansonniers* (Liège, 1991), pp. 85–217.

55 *Testi didattico-cortesi di Provenza*, ed. Giuseppe E. Sansone (Bari, 1977), pp. 53–74.

surviving source for this work.[56] The author proposes practical instruc-
tions for the comportment of a damsel in various circumstances at
court. Following his praise of "courtesy," understood as the sum of those
qualities that must characterize everyone at court, he offers the damsel
this advice:

> *Ioglars e chantadors,*
> *que paraula[n] d'amors*
> *e cantons sons e lais,*
> *per que l'om es plus gais,*
> *e meton en corage*
> *de tot prez vassallage,*
> *retenez amoros.*

> Jongleurs and singers—
> who speak of love
> and sing melodies and lais,
> which make one more cheerful;
> and who bring to the spirit
> a desire for perfect worthiness—
> you must entertain with affection.

Like the lord of the castle, she too is obliged to demonstrate her generosity, that essential component of courtesy:

> *Se quer aver de vos,*
> *o ab dar vostr'aver*
> *o ab altre placer,*
> *lor faiz tan bella enseigna*
> *per que talanz lor preigna*
> *qe diga de vos be.*

> If they ask money of you,
> or for your liberal offering
> or for other gifts,
> give them such fine demonstration
> that they will desire
> to speak well of you.

With their poetic and musical art they will then carry the fame of their
benefactress far and wide:

---

56   Berlin, Deutsche Staatsbibliothek, MS Phillips, 1910.

Ab que no·n sapchaz re,
vostre noms n'er saupuz
e plus loing mentauguz:
en molz locs n'aureç preç
qu'eissa vos non saureç.

Though you may know nothing of it,
your name will become known
and celebrated afar:
you will become famous in many places
of which you yourself will be unaware.

Even as the thirteenth century drew to a close, images of Provençal poetry and music were still alive in Italy. One story in the *Novellino*[57] opens with this description of the Provençal court of Puy-de-Notre-Dame:

> *I cavalieri e' donzelli, ch'erano giulivi e gai, si faceano di belle canzoni e 'l suono*
> *e 'l motto; e quattro approvatori erano stabiliti, che quelle ch'aveano valore*
> *faceano mettere in conto e, l'altre, diceano, a chi l'avea fatte, che le migliorasse.*

The knights and damsels, who were merry and cheerful, created both the words and music of beautiful chansons; and four arbiters were chosen, who would accredit those that were worthy, while they said of the others, to those who created them, that they should be improved.

A subsequent passage in the story draws much of its material from the *vida* of Rigaut de Berbezilh and the *razo* of his chanson *Atressi com l'olifant:*[58]

> *cominciò questa sua canzonetta tanto soavemente quanto seppe il meglio, ché*
> *molto il sapea ben fare:*
>> *Atressi come il leofante*
>> *quando cade non si può levare ...*

he began this his chansonnette as sweetly as could possibly be, so capable of many things was he:

> Just as the elephant
> who cannot rise when it falls ...

Rigaut de Berbezilh never traveled to Italy himself, but his poetry and music did. The chanson, translated into Italian here in the *Novellino*,

---

57 *Il "Novellino,"* ed. Guido Favati (Genoa, 1970), pp. 269–75.

58 Rigaut de Berbezilh, *Liriche*, ed. Alberto Varvaro (Bari, 1960); music in *Las cançons*, pp. 72–82.

appears in the Veneto music codex, though the melody is significantly different from the one surviving in two French chansonniers:

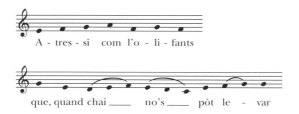

We know from Francesco da Barberino and Dante that Provençal poetry was still widely known and highly regarded in Italian culture in the early fourteenth century; but the same does not seem to hold for the music originally accompanying those texts. Though Francesco da Barberino mentioned various troubadours who had come to Italy, such as Peire Vidal, Gaucelm Faidit, and Aimeric de Pegulhan, he left no indication whatsoever of having heard their music.[59] Even his observation regarding poetry adapted to preexisting instrumental dance melodies ("inventio verborum que supra aliquo caribo, nota, stampita vel similibus componebatur precompositis sonis"[new words that are composed to go with some previously composed *caribo, nota, stampita,* or such])[60] could simply have been based on the *razo* of *Calenda maia,* which survives in only one manuscript that was copied in his same epoch and area.[61]

Of the "illustres cantiones" Dante cited as models of poetic structure, one alone, by Folquet de Marseille,[62] has come down to us with its music:

the loving thought is so pleasing to me.

Dante most certainly admired its textual *constructio* based on the solemn meter of *endecasillabi,* but it is doubtful whether his admiration included

59   Antoine Thomas, *Francesco da Barberino et la littérature provençale en Italie au Moyen Age* (Paris, 1883), pp. 103 ff.

60   Francesco da Barberino, *I documenti d'amore,* ed. Francesco Egidi, vol. 2 (Rome, 1927), p. 263.

61   See note 7 to this chapter.

62   *Le troubadour Folquet de Marseille,* ed. Stanislaw Stronski (Cracow, 1910); music in *Las cançons,* pp. 187–227.

the music. Further, we can see here how the cultural status of the poetry was very different from that of the music. The first line of the text, for instance, seems to have possessed an unusual fascination for poets of the time. Sordello used it for a text of his own, in the same meter:

Tant m'abelis lo terminis novels.

And Dante used it as well, to begin the tercets in Provençal spoken by Arnaut Daniel in Purgatory:

Tan m'abelis vostre cortes deman.

It seems unlikely that the initial phrase of the music, a formula common to nearly all of Folquet's melodic settings, would have been as fascinating as the text. Even though the entire chanson was later appropriated to become the second voice of a French motet (with text in translation), this polyphonic composition perhaps never made its way as far as Italy.[63]

Dante might well have encountered the music of the troubadours at the court of Cangrande della Scala in Verona. It was here that Fazio degli Uberti (at a relatively late date, in the mid-fourteenth century) had included Provençal verses in his *Dittamondo*.[64] It would also seem to have been the last bastion of Provençal poetry and music, perhaps responsible for the only such music codex we know to have been copied in Italy (a document dating from the early fourteenth century and generally identified as originating in the Lombardy-Veneto region). According to Immanuel Romano, all requisite etiquette could be found at the court of Cangrande.[65] There was homage to the lord:

e questo è 'l signore
con tanto valore
che 'l suo grande onore
va per terra e mare.

and this is the lord
so valorous
that his great honor
travels over land and sea.

---

63   Ziino, "Caratteri e significato," p. 206 n. 72.

64   Fazio degli Uberti, *Il "Dittamondo e le rime,"* ed. Giuseppe Corsi, vol. 1 (Bari, 1952), pp. 314–15.

65   *Rimatori comico-realistici del Due e Trecento*, ed. Maurizio Vitale, vol. 2 (Turin, 1956), pp. 103–12.

There were knights and armaments:

> *Destriere e corsiere*
> *masnate e bandiere*
> *corazze e lamiere*
> *vedrai remutare.*

> Steeds and chargers,
> guards and standards,
> armor and steel
> always fresh you will see.

There were women and amours:

> *Qui vengon poi fate,*
> *con le bionde teste:*
> *qui son le tempeste*
> *d'amore e d'amare.*

> Here too are enchanting beauties,
> with their heads of blonde:
> here there are tempests
> of love and of loving.

There was music of instruments and voices:

> *Chitarre e liuti*
> *viole e flauti,*
> *voci alt'ed acute*
> *qui s'odon cantare.*

> Guitars and lutes,
> vielles and flutes,
> voices high and bright
> here are heard sounding.

And still, at that time:

> *Qui boni cantori*
> *con intonatori*
> *e qui* trovatori
> *udrai concordare.*

> Here fine singers
> with improvisors,
> and here *troubadours*
> you will hear in accord.

Two

THE VISCONTI
LIBRARY

I

Jacopo da Bologna wrote two madrigals and perhaps two motets in honor of Luchino Visconti, lord of Milan from 1339 to 1349.[1] The motet *Lux purpurata radiis—Diligite justitiam* for the most part pays tribute to Luchino's civic and military virtues, but at least one line, "constans in omni studio" (persevering in every study) may allude to his literary interests. Luchino was fond of poetry, even exchanging sonnets on the theme of princely generosity with Fazio degli Uberti (who visited Luchino's court and wrote verses in honor of his son Brizio and his nephews and eventual successors Bernabò and Galeazzo II).[2] He was also the first of his family to collect books. Among the volumes carrying his mark of ownership is a codex containing the treatise *De electionibus* by the French canonist Guillaume de Mandagout (A 480),[3] early evidence of the particular interest the Visconti court would have for ultramontane culture. Another French author, Philippe de Mézières, was at Luchino's court in 1345, and he later chronicled events regarding Bernabò and Giangaleazzo as well.[4] French music

---

1   F. Alberto Gallo, *La polifonia nel Medioevo* (Turin, 1991), pp. 65–69; English edition, *Music of the Middle Ages II* (Cambridge, 1985), pp. 56–61.

2   Fazio degli Uberti, *Il "Dittamondo e le rime,"* ed. Giuseppe Corsi, vol. 2 (Bari, 1952), pp. 43–48.

3   Parenthetical inventory number refers to Élizabeth Pellegrin, *La bibliothèque des Visconti et des Sforza ducs de Milan au XVe siècle* (Paris, 1955), pp. 75–289 (inventory A, nos. 1–988).

4   Philippe de Mézières, *Le songe du vieil pèlerin*, ed. George William Coopland, vol. 1 (Cambridge, 1969), pp. 4, 149, 151, 281–83, 605.

was also influential at Luchino's court: when Jacopo da Bologna mentioned "Filippi e Marchetti" in one of his madrigals for Luchino,[5] he was referring to the French composer and theorist Philippe de Vitry and the Italian composer and theorist Marchetto da Padova.

As court musician, Jacopo not only rendered homage to his lord, but he also described the activities organized at Luchino's court to pass the time:

> *Per sparverare tolsi el mio sparvero*
> *brachi e brache chiamando.*[6]

> To go hunting I freed my hawk,
> calling the male and female hounds.

This is the beginning of a musical caccia[7] whose text describes a hunting episode. The name of one of the hounds, "Varin," appears in the text of another caccia (set to music by Piero and Giovanni, two musicians who were probably also present at court) that describes a Visconti hunt:

> *Con bracchi assai e con molti sparveri*
> *uccellavam su per la riva d'Ada.*[8]

> With sundry hounds and with many hawks
> we hunted birds along the banks of the Adda.

These images bring to mind the Visconti reputation for their fine birds of prey and the "multas bonas bracas" (many good hounds) they would procure from the Gonzagas of Mantua, and their hunting reserve bordered by the Po, Ticino, and Adda rivers.[9] The books they acquired also reflect this passion for the hunt: such as the two copies of the treatise *De avibus* by Hugh of Fouilloy (A 733, 745), which contains the chapter "de accipitre,"[10] on the hawk of the caccia; and the copy of the *Tractatus de*

---

5 *Poesie musicali del Trecento,* ed. Giuseppe Corsi (Bologna, 1970), p. 42.

6 Ibid., pp. 52–53.

7 CACCIA: a lively canon, usually about hunting or village scenes, often using sounds such as beggars' cries or the barking of dogs.

8 Corsi, *Poesie musicali,* p. 9.

9 Carlo Magenta, *I Visconti e gli Sforza nel castello di Pavia* (Milan, 1883), vol. 1, pp. 117–28; vol. 2, pp. 26–33, 51.

10 *Patrologiae cursus completus, series latina* (PL), ed. Jacques Paul Migne, vol. 177 (Paris, 1879), cols. 13–55.

medicina et naturis falchionum (A 433), attributed to a mythical king Dancus, which deals extensively with falcons and hawks.[11]

Luchino's son Brizio was himself to become a renowned collector of books: "morales librosque undique aquirebat" (and he acquired from everywhere books pertaining to morals) was written of him.[12] He owned at least one copy of the *Compendium moralis philosophie*, dedicated to him by the Dominican Luca Mannelli (A 132), and a copy of *De civitate Dei* by Saint Augustine (A 166). Brizio was also a poet of some talent. In one of his canzoni, dedicated to the women of Florence, there is a musical reminiscence suggestive of Dante:

> *E poi mi parve udir più dolci suoni,*
> *cantar mi parvon tutti "In alto osanna."*[13]

> And then I seemed to hear the sweetest sounds;
> all seemed to be singing "Hosanna on high."

Between 1353 and 1356 Bartolomeo di Bartoli da Bologna wrote *La canzone delle virtù e delle scienze* for Brizio, and Nicolò da Bologna decorated it with miniatures.[14] Naturally Music is described and illustrated as one of the sciences. The poem refers to such activities as dance—"per lei se balla e salta" (because of [Music] one dances and leaps)—and such aesthetic motivations as pleasure—"e sa d'ogne alegreza i chori infundere" (and [Music] can infuse hearts with every sort of happiness)—that were relevant to court life. Music's pictorial representation is also set in a courtly context: a young woman, elegantly dressed, is singing and accompanying herself on a stringed instrument— a "chitarra," as Fazio degli Uberti wrote with reference to the inventor of music:

> *Iubal, suo frate, trovò modo al canto*
> *ad organi e chitarra . . .*[15]

> Jubal, his brother, discovered how to sing
> with the organ and guitar . . .

---

11   *Dancus Rex, Guilelmus Falconarius, Gerardus Falconarius: Les plus anciens traités de fauconnerie de l'occident,* ed. Gunnar Tilander (Lund, 1963).

12   Pietro Azario, *Liber gestorum in Lombardia,* ed. Francesco Cognasso (Bologna, 1939), p. 44.

13   *Rimatori del Trecento,* ed. Giuseppe Corsi (Turin, 1969), pp. 197–98.

14   Bartolomeo di Bartoli da Bologna, *La canzone delle virtù e delle scienze,* ed. Léon Dorez (Bergamo, 1904).

15   Degli Uberti, *Il "Dittamondo,"* vol. 1, p. 450.

Jubal or Tubal or Tubalcain is present in this miniature as well, hammering an anvil at the woman's feet, and there are two columns engraved with notes and intervals, the essential elements of the art; both were traditional components in the visual representation of Music. Certainly no reader at the Visconti court would have had any trouble interpreting these iconographic details: the library contained no less than four exemplars of the *Historia scolastica* by Petrus Comestor (A 228, 325, 326, 594), which narrates that Tubalcain preserved the music he invented by engraving the essential elements on two columns—one made of marble, resistant to water, and the other of clay, resistant to fire.[16]

With the deaths first of Luchino Visconti in 1349 and then of his brother Giovanni (who also collected books)[17] in 1354, dynastic power was partitioned among their three nephews Bernabò, Matteo II, and Galeazzo II. Matteo died in 1355, and Bernabò and Galeazzo established their courts in Milan and Pavia respectively. The only book known to have belonged to Bernabò is a copy of the *Liber iudiciorum et consiliorum* by Alfodhol da Merengi (A 203), which carries Bernabò's emblem and motto: a serpent with a youth in its mouth, a leopard, and the French motto "Soffrir m'estuet" (I must suffer). These same particulars are described in the text of a contemporary madrigal in three languages, Italian-Latin-French, possibly by Petrarch:[18]

> *La fiera testa che d'uman si ciba*
> *pennis auratis volitum perquirit*
>
> . . .
>
> *Cist fier cimiers est la flamme che m'art*
> Soffrir m'estuet *che son fier leopart.*[19]

16   PL 198, col. 1079.

17   Élizabeth Pellegrin, "Notes sur deux nouveaux manuscrits des Visconti et des Sforza de Milan," in *Bibliothèques retrouvées: Manuscrits, bibliothèques et bibliophiles du Moyen Age et de la Renaissance* (Paris, 1988), pp. 399–401.

18   Élizabeth Pellegrin, *La bibliothèque des Visconti et des Sforza ducs de Milan au XVe siècle: Supplément* (Florence and Paris, 1969), pp. 28–29; and Geneviève Thibault, "Emblèmes et devises des Visconti dans les oeuvres musicales du Trecento," *L'ars nova italiana del Trecento* (1970): 150–52.

19   Corsi, *Poesie musicali*, pp. 96–97.

The proud head that feeds on a human,
seeks flight with golden feathers
. . .
This proud insignia is the flame that ignites me,
Soffrir m'estuet, I am a proud leopard.

Two polyphonic, mensurally notated settings of this text (by Nicolò da Perugia and Bartolino da Padova) would seem to reflect the level of written composition that had been reached at Bernabò's court. Certainly there was a great deal and a great variety of musical activity going on. Historical accounts make a point of mentioning that even during a military campaign Bernabò found a way to pass some time "cum cantis et musicis" (with songs and music).[20] One of the more noteworthy performing figures at his court was Dolcibene, who is described in *Il Paradiso degli Alberti* as follows:

> *Messer Dolcibene . . . essendo bello di corpo, robusto, gagliardo e convenevole musico e sonatore di organetti, di leuto e d'altri stromenti, udito la fama e la felicità di Messer Bernabò e messer Galeazzo Visconti di Melano e della loro onorata e magnifica corte, diliberò andarne per avanzare sua vita là; e così fè. Dove e' fu bene accettato e veduto per le sue virtù, facendo sue canzonette in rittimi con parole molto piacevoli e intonandole con dolcissimi canti, per la qual cosa molti doni ricevea da molti gentili uomini e signori che in quelli tempi nella detta corte trovavansi.[21]*

> Master Dolcibene . . . being handsome, robust, vigorous, and a proper musician and player of portative organs, the lute, and other instruments, and having heard of the fame and magnanimity of Master Bernabò and Master Galeazzo Visconti of Milan, and of their honored and magnificent court, decided to go seek his fortune there; and so he did. There he was well received and highly esteemed for his virtues, creating his canzonette in meters with very pleasant words and setting them to sweet melodies, for which he received many gifts from many gentlemen and lords who were at the court at that time.

Dolcibene was a great friend of Franco Sacchetti and the protagonist of many of his stories (in one of them Bernabò also appears, as does,

---

20 Conforto da Costozza, *Frammenti di storia vicentina,* ed. Carlo Steiner (Città di Castello, 1915), p. 17.

21 Giovanni Gherardi da Prato, *Il Paradiso degli Alberti,* ed. Antonio Lanza (Rome, 1975), pp. 201–2.

fleetingly, the musical madrigal).[22] What remains of Dolcibene's poetry ranges from bawdy jokes in sonnets he exchanged with Sacchetti[23] to a pious description of his journey to the Holy Land, where he sang the *Te Deum* in the Valley of Yosefat and the *Credo* on Mount Ascension.[24]

Bernabò and Galeazzo II had spent their youth in Savoy and in France (exiled by their uncle Luchino), an experience that reinforced the already firm Visconti ties with French culture. These ties were even further strengthened when Galeazzo II married Blanche of Savoy in 1350. Galeazzo continued the traditional Visconti interest in books, commissioning many of his acquisitions (some of which were decorated with his portrait),[25] and providing a repository for them with the institution of a genuine court library (a room on the upper floor of the front left tower) in the castle he built in Pavia between 1360 and 1365.[26]

Petrarch was in Pavia between 1354 and 1361. During this period he began work on *De remediis utriusque fortune,* later dedicating it to Azzo da Correggio—a figure like few others at the mercy of fickle fortune—who died at Galeazzo's court in 1366. The library at Pavia possessed no fewer than five copies of *De remediis* (A 386, 391, 633, 837, 965). The work consists of a series of dialogues conducted by "Ratio," with "Gaudium" in the first part and with "Dolor" in the second, on various aspects of the human condition. Two contiguous dialogues in the first part, which is the only place appropriate for the subject of music, deal with the two aspects that it could assume at court: accompanied song and dance. In dialogue 23, the interventions of "Gaudium," which "Ratio" attempts to oppose with negative or at least restrictive arguments, are the following nine:

> *Cantu delector ac fidibus.*
> *Cantibus sonisque permulceor.*
> *Musica suavitate delinior.*
> *Cantu gaudeo et exaltor.*
> *Cano dulciter.*

22   Franco Sacchetti, *Il "Trecentonovelle,"* ed. Antonio Lanza (Florence, 1984), novellas 10, 24, 25, 33, 117, 153, 156, 187, and 74.

23   Franco Sacchetti, *Il libro delle rime,* ed. Francesca Brambilla Ageno (Florence, 1990), pp. 149–50.

24   *Rime pie edite e inedite di messer Dolcibene,* ed. Giovanni Tortoli (Florence, 1904).

25   Élizabeth Pellegrin, "Portraits de Galéas II Visconti seigneur de Milan (1378)," in *Bibliothèques retrouvées,* pp. 367–69.

26   Carlo Magenta, *I Visconti e gli Sforza nel castello di Pavia* (Milan, 1883), vol. 1, pp. 74–92.

Cantu ac tibiis delector.
Cantu moveor.
Delectat canere.
Suavibus vocum modis cum delectatione detineor.

I delight in song and the music of stringed instruments.
I am charmed by songs and sounds.
I am soothed by pleasant music.
I enjoy song and am uplifted by it.
I sing sweetly.
I delight in song and the music of the pipes.
Song moves me.
It is pleasant to sing.
Voices singing sweet songs transfix me with delight.[27]

Music is indicated generically only in the third statement; in all other cases it is specified as vocal music—accompanied by instruments in the second line, by stringed instruments in the first line, by wind instruments in the sixth line, as polyphony, most probably, in the ninth line. It is song that captivates and moves (lines 4 and 7), song not only heard but also personally performed (lines 5 and 8). In dialogue 24 the interventions of "Gaudium," always promptly countered by "Ratio," are the following six:

Choreis gaudeo.
Choreis cupide intersum.
Dulcedinem quandam ex choreis capio.
Choreis delector.
Delectabiles sunt choree.
Honesto tripudio libenter exerceo.

I enjoy dancing.
I eagerly take part in dances.
I obtain a certain pleasure from dancing.
I delight in dancing.
Dances are delightful.
I gladly exercise with wholesome dancing.

Dance brings enjoyment, pleasure, delight (lines 1, 3, 4, 5); and while the simple spectator is not entirely excluded, it seems clear that such effects are primarily the result of direct participation in the art (lines 2 and 6).

---

27 Translation adapted from Conrad H. Rawski, "Petrarch's Dialogue on Music," *Speculum* 46 (1971): 302–17.

Galeazzo II died in 1378, leaving his son Giangaleazzo to succeed him. Seven years later the younger Visconti had his uncle Bernabò imprisoned and killed, thereby becoming the sole ruler over all of Lombardy. His marriage in 1360 to Isabelle, daughter of King John II of France, had brought to Giangaleazzo in dowry the county of Vertus in Champagne, whence the encomiastic appellation "conte di Virtù" (count of Virtue, or Valor) by which he was known in Italy. Two instrumental dances ("istampite," from the French "estampie"), entitled respectively "Isabella" and "Virtù," were probably written in celebration of this marriage.[28]

Giangaleazzo's political, dynastic, and cultural relationships with the French court, always extremely important for him, reached their zenith in 1387 when his daughter Valentina was wed to Louis of Orléans, brother of Charles VI. The castle library at Pavia (whose holdings increased considerably in this period, thanks to the personal attention of Giangaleazzo and his secretary Pasquino Cappelli) was significantly affected by this general situation, with ultramontane culture becoming a prominent feature among its many volumes (nearly one thousand are listed in an inventory taken in 1426).[29]

There were collections of verses by Arnaut de Mereuil (A 298), Giraut de Bornelh (A 407), and Peire Cardenal (A 412), proof that the courts of northern Italy long maintained their interest in Provençal poetry.[30] Examples of French literature ranged from *Roman de la Rose* (A 900) to *Dit du Lion* by Guillaume de Machaut (A 889). There were also two codices that seem to reflect a certain attention to French music of the period: one was an exemplar of *Renart le Nouvel* by Jaquemart le Gélee (A 300), a romance in verse from the end of the thirteenth century containing numerous musical interpolations;[31] and the other a book "cum notis musicis" (with musical notation) that began with the composition *Apta caro* and must therefore have been a collection of French motets from the first half of

28   Timothy J. McGee, *Medieval Instrumental Dances* (Bloomington and Indianapolis, 1989), pp. 79–83, 102–6.

29   Antoine Thomas, "Les manuscrits français et provençaux des Ducs de Milan au Chateau de Pavie," *Romania* 40 (1911): 571–609.

30   See chapter 1.

31   Maria C. Coldwell, "Guillaume de Dole and Medieval Romances with Musical Interpolations," *Musica disciplina* 35 (1981): 73.

the fourteenth century.[32] Still another book of music could have been in some way connected to the Visconti court, since it had been copied at Pavia in this general period: it contains music treatises both Italian (Marchetto da Padova) and French (Philippe de Vitry), and a French composition, *La harpe de mélodie,* by Jacob de Senleches. The copyist, one "G. de Anglia" (English visitors were not rare: Chaucer, for example, was often at Pavia during the years 1368–78), completed this manuscript in October 1391.[33]

In March of that same year a group of French nobles, among them Louis of Orléans (husband of Valentina Visconti) and the duke of Burgundy, were guests of Giangaleazzo in his castle at Pavia. Accompanying them was Eustache Déschamps, the poet disciple of Machaut (Giangaleazzo would later try to bring the poetess Christine de Pisan to his court as well). Déschamps left a description of that visit in verse,[34] which begins

> *Il fait tresbeau demourer*
> *en doulz chastel de Pavie.*

> It is lovely to live
> in the gentle castle of Pavia.

There is also mention of court festivities:

> *car c'est noble compaignie*
> *et qui dance voluntiers*

> because there is a noble company
> who dances with pleasure

and the ability of the ladies to dance and sing:

> *dancer scevent et chanter*
> *doucement . . .*

> they knew how to dance and to sing
> sweetly . . .

---

32   F. Alberto Gallo, "Per un repertorio delle fonti perdute," *Schede medievali* 3 (1982): 291.

33   Kurt von Fischer, "Eine wiederaufgefundene Theoretikerhandschrift des späten 14. Jahrhunderts," *Schweizer Beiträge zur Musikwissenschaft* 1 (1972): 23–33.

34   *Oeuvres complètes de Eustache Deschamps,* ed. Le Marquis de Queux de Saint-Hilaire, vol. 5 (Paris, 1887), pp. 314–16.

This might well have been when *La harpe de mélodie* was written.[35] In the Pavia codex the musical notation for this *ballade* uses the strings of a harp depicted on the page, rather than the usual five-line staff. As the text states, it was conceived to be both a parlor game "pour plaire une compaignie" (to entertain a company; perhaps the "noble compaignie" of Deschamps?) and a show of skill (what erudite, bookish music indeed!) in creating harmony to "oir, sonner et veir" (hear, play, and behold).

The harp was the favorite instrument at the court of Pavia, the instrument that Valentina Visconti played.[36] It therefore enjoys considerable attention in a chansonnier by Francesco di Vannozzo, poet-musician at Giangaleazzo's court from 1389. Within this chansonnier is a group of sonnets that Francesco styled as an exchange with his lute, which he would use to accompany himself as he sang.[37] One tenso begins with the lute reproaching Francesco for neglect:

> *Haimi lassato per diletto d'arpa.*

> You have abandoned me for the pleasures of a harp.

In another of his sonnets the harp is the protagonist:[38]

> *Il tuo fratel Francesco a te mi manda.*

> Your brother Francesco sends me to you.

Here the French origin of this instrument is emphasized,

> *m'ha tratto fuor del bel pays de Franza*

> he brought me hither from the beautiful land of France

as is its superiority over all other instruments:

> *arpa mi chiamo per antica usanza*
> *che sopra ogni altro suon porto ghirlanda.*

---

35   Reinhard Strohm, "*La harpe de mélodie* oder das Kunstwerk als Akt der Zueignung," in *Das musikalische Kunstwerk: Geschichte, Aestetik, Theorie (Festschrift Carl Dahlhaus)* (Laaber, 1988), pp. 305–16.

36   André Pirro, *La musique à Paris sous le règne de Charles VI, 1380–1422* (Strasbourg, 1930), pp. 12–13.

37   *Le rime di Francesco di Vannozzo*, ed. Antonio Medin (Bologna, 1928), p. 52.

38   Ibid., pp. 58–59.

I am called a harp by ancient custom,
and my sound is prized above all others.

Francesco's harp is also a "harpe de mélodie":

io ti farò sentir tal melodia
che l'alma tua serà sempre rifatta.

I will have you hear such a fine melody
that your spirit will be always restored.

There must certainly have been an exemplar of the chansonnier in the Visconti library, since it is in a sense dedicated to Giangaleazzo: it closes with a "cantilena . . . pro comite Virtutum" (song . . . for the count of Virtue),[39] and it opens with a "canzon morale fatta per la divisa del conte di Virtù" (moral canzone written for the heraldic device of the count of Virtue).[40] This introductory canzone describes the emblem and motto created by Petrarch for Giangaleazzo on the occasion of his marriage to Isabelle of France: a white turtledove within a sun emanating golden rays, and the French motto "A bon droyt" (with good reason; by right). Books commissioned by Giangaleazzo would often incorporate these hallmarks: for example, on the page reproduced in figure 11, there are four such emblems around the large initial letter "E," while the motto (partially Italianized) is spelled out around the perimeter: beginning on the upper left side and continuing down and along the bottom sides are the letters for "a buon," while the top and right sides provide the letters for "droyt." The motto also appears in a circular pattern in the left margin, and again within the body of the "E," in its left side. The miniature itself is a musical scene; thus we have an example where emblem, motto, and music are brought together for the illustration of a book. These same three elements are even more tightly and functionally grouped in a contemporary musical composition with the following descriptive French text:

Le ray au soleyl qui dret son karmeyne
en soy braçant la douce tortorelle
. . .
A bon droyt *semble que en toy perfect regne.*[41]

39   Ibid., pp. 266–75.
40   Ibid., pp. 3–14.
41   *The Works of Johannes Ciconia,* ed. Margaret Bent and Anne Hallmark, in *Polyphonic Music of the Fourteenth Century,* vol. 24 (Monaco, 1985), pp. 177–78.

> The sun ray which leads a correct melody,
> the sweet turtle dove rocking herself,
>
> . . .
>
> it seems that *a bon droyt,* perfection reigns in you.

The Visconti court looked to France not only as a source of musical and literary interest and fashion, but also as a model of etiquette and ceremonial practices. In the library at Pavia there was a prose version of the *Ordre de Chévalerie* (A 858), and a volume described as an "ordinarium tenendum in capella regia coperto corio rubeo sculpto ad modum parisinum" (ordinal to be kept in the royal chapel, with red leather binding carved in the Parisian manner) (A 912), which must have been the ceremonial book of the French royal chapel. French court festivities were also emulated. When Charles VI married Isabelle of Bavaria in 1389, there were several days of celebration in Paris that involved, after the religious ceremony, a grand banquet with musical intermezzi, the presentation of the gifts, and various tournaments and balls,[42] reflecting a thoroughly organized structure that would remain in fashion for centuries to come. Giangaleazzo readily adopted it for his investiture as duke of Milan in 1395. On Sunday, 10 September, after the solemn religious ceremony, there was a great banquet with each course presented to the strident sound of trumpets ("quodlibet ferculum associat tibicinum ingens stridor"); "the remainder of that day was spent in group dances and leaping dances" ("reliquum diei illius choreis et tripudiis consumatur"); and the following day there were jousting tournaments.[43] The text of a madrigal by Antonello da Caserta perhaps refers to these festivities. It begins

> *Del glorioso titol d'esto duce,*
> *çascun fa fest' omai, ch'à in sé vertute*

> With the glorious title of this leader,
> all now rejoice for him who possesses virtue

and goes on to mention "triumfi e feste" (pageants and festivities).[44] No doubt Pietro da Castelleto was amply justified when, in his funeral oration

---

42   *Chroniques de Froissart,* ed. Kervyn de Lettenhove, vol. 14 (Brussels, 1872), pp. 15–24.
43   Francesco Arisio, *Cremona literata,* vol. 1 (Parma, 1702), p. 198.
44   *The Lucca Codex,* ed. John Nádas and Agostino Ziino (Lucca, 1990), p. 38.

for Giangaleazzo (A 938), he mentioned "spectacula, cantus et epule" (spectacles, singing, and banquets) as he recalled some of the many splendors of the Visconti court.[45]

II

Libellus de ludo scacorum is the title of a book that was present in multiple copies in the Visconti library (A 257, 258, 261, 874, 886). Two other important fourteenth-century court libraries (which may have been models for the Visconti one), those of King Charles V of France,[46] and of his brother Jean, duke of Berry,[47] possessed respectively five copies (533–37) and one exemplar (172). Written by the Dominican friar Giacomo da Cessole toward the end of the thirteenth century,[48] the work was not so much a manual for the game of chess as an interpretation of chess as an allegory of the hierarchical and functional arrangement of secular society. The first section of the treatise is dedicated to the "scachi nobiles" (noble chess ranks), the king and queen and the other court-related pieces; the second section addresses "de formis et officiis scachorum popularium" (the forms and functions of the popular ranks). In this latter section the eight pawns represent various categories of workers: farmers, craftsmen, wool workers, physicians and pharmacist-cosmeticians, merchants, innkeepers, guards, and messengers. The pawn for the category "medici et pigmentarii" (physicians and cosmeticians), which is positioned in front of the queen, is in the form of a man seated with a book in his right hand. The author explains that the book stands for "omnes grammatici, loyci, rethorici, geometrici, arismetrici, musici et astronomi" (all grammarians, logicians, rhetoricians, geometers, arithmeticians, musicians, and astronomers)— that is, all those educated in the system of the seven "artes liberales."[49] This kind of "scholastic" legitimation clearly explains the presence of a certain type of "music" in the court library.

45   *Rerum italicarum scriptores*, ed. Ludovico A. Muratori, vol. 16 (Milan, 1730), col. 1049.

46   Leopold Delisle, *Recherches sur la librairie de Charles V, roi de France, 1337–1380*, vol. 2 (Paris, 1907), pp. 3–200 (inventory nos. 1–1239).

47   Ibid., pp. 223–318 (inventory nos. 1–296).

48   Thomas Käppeli, *Scriptores ordinis praedicatorum medii aevii*, vol. 2 (Rome, 1975), pp. 311–17.

49   Paris, Bibliothèque Nationale, MS latin 6705, fol. 28v.

The library at Pavia possessed a nearly complete collection of the principal scholastic manuals of ancient, high medieval, and contemporary culture, which all included a section on music. From Greek literature there
was one exemplar of Plato's *Timaeus* in the original Greek, formerly
belonging to Petrarch (A 120); there were also three exemplars of it in
Latin translation with commentary, by Calcidio (A 30, 121, 123) (one copy
was also in the library of Charles V [476]). From Latin literature there
were exemplars of *De architectura* by Vitruvius (A 254) and the *Institutio ora-
toria* by Quintilian (A 656). From early medieval literature were those
works that established the system of the seven liberal arts, with music as
one of the disciplines of the "quadrivium": one copy of *De nuptiis Philologie
et Mercurii* by Martianus Capella (A 39) and one of *De institutione secularium
litterarum* by Cassiodorus (A 181), which Petrarch had commissioned for
himself, with miniatures representing the seven arts;[50] three copies of the
Etymologie by Isidore of Seville (A 100, 103, 167); and one of the *De institutione musica* by Boethius (A 555). From more recent medieval literature
there was one exemplar each of the *Didascalion* by Hugh of St. Victor (A
81) and the *Liber excerptionum* by Richard of St. Victor (A 687), and three
of the *Polycraticus* by John of Salisbury (A 81, 172, 635) (two also in the
library of Charles V [500–501]); five exemplars of the *Anticlaudianus* by
Alain de Lille (A 40, 41, 44, 54, 81 (one also in the library of Charles V
[1080]); and two exemplars of *De proprietatibus rerum* by Bartholomaeus
Anglicus (A 145, 222) (six—two of them in French translation—also in
the library of Charles V [439–44] and five in the library of the duke of
Berry [142–46]).

Still with regard to the eighth pawn, the author of the *Ludus scacorum*
went on to assert that "perfectus medicus phisicus novit . . . armoniam pul-
suum tamquam quandam armoniam musice" (a skillful doctor knows . . .
the harmony of the pulses like the harmony of music).[51] Thus there was a
"scientific" legitimation for the presence of another type of "music" in the
court library.

---

50   Paris, Bibliothèque Nationale, MS latin 8500, fol. 39v; *Dix siècles d'enluminure italienne
(VIe–XVIe siècle)*, ed. François Avril (Paris, 1984), pp. 85–86 and table XI.
51   Paris, Bibliothèque Nationale, MS latin 6705, fol. 28v.

The library at Pavia had a rich collection of scientific works, translated or elaborated in a court environment, that included the consideration of music. Among them were the following:

One exemplar of *Tacuinum sanitatis* (A 482) (one also in the library of Charles V [843]). The original Arabic of this treatise, a series of tables on medicine and hygiene, had been compiled in the first half of the eleventh century by Ibn Botlan, a Christian physician from Baghdad. The Latin translation seems to have been done at the court of Manfred, son of Frederick II, who ruled Sicily between 1253 and 1259.[52] Music appears as the subject of one of the tables because, as the introduction states, "musice sunt instrumenta iuvativa ad conservandam sanitatem et amissam restituendam iuxta diversitates complexionum hominum" (music is a means that can be used as an aid in maintaining or restoring health, according to people's various constitutions). There is a tripartite division of music, into "cantus" (singing), "organare cantum vel sonare" (accompanying a song or playing music), and "sonare et saltare" (playing music and dancing).[53]

Two exemplars of the commentary by Campano da Novara (active at the papal court in the second half of the thirteenth century) for the Latin translation of Euclid's *Elements* (A 255, 256) (one also in the library of Charles V [550]), the fifth book of which discusses the "proportiones." It would appear that there was particular interest in the subject of proportions at the Visconti court. Biagio Pelacani, who taught at the University of Pavia (founded by Galeazzo II) between 1375 and 1404, seems to have been the author of a treatise on proportions that included a discussion of music;[54] and there is a *Tabula super proportiones* by Albert of Saxony[55] on the page facing *La harpe de mélodie* in the volume of music copied in Pavia in 1391 that was discussed above. This interest would tie in with the application of proportions to temporal measurement, which first surfaces in the works of

52   Hosam Elkhadem, "Tacuini sanitatis: A Little-Known Edition of 1531," *LIAS* 1 (1974): 119–28.

53   F. Alberto Gallo, "La trattistica musicale," in *Storia della cultura veneta* (Vicenza, 1981), vol. 3/III, pp. 307–8 and fig. 75.

54   John E. Murdoch, "Music and Natural Philosophy: Hitherto Unnoticed Quaestiones by Blasius of Parma(?)," *Manuscripta* 20 (1976): 119–36.

55   Hubertus Lambertus Ludovicus Busard, "Der *Tractatus proportionum* von Albert von Sachsen," *Denkschriften der österreichischen Akademie der Wissenschaften, mathematische-naturwissenschaftliche Klasse* 116, no. 2 (1971): 43–72.

certain composers thought to have been active at Pavia, such as Filippotto
da Caserta.[56] The measurement of time was in any case a fixed physical presence in the castle library, where a place of honor was reserved for a marvelous object of fourteenth-century calculation, a clock constructed by Giovanni Dondi[57] (Dondi was, incidentally, a poet as well, whose work was set to
music by the "Visconti" musician Bartolino da Padova).

One exemplar of the treatise on astronomy by Michael Scot (A 112),
written at the court of Frederick II.[58] One exemplar of the *Problems,* attributed to Aristotle (A 109), in the Latin translation by Bartolomeo da
Messina for Manfred, king of Sicily[59] (one also in the library of Charles V
[472]; while in the library of the duke of Berry there was an exemplar of
the French translation with commentary by Evrart de Conty [153], physician to Charles V). Three copies of a commentary, again on the *Problems,*
by Pietro da Abano (A 150, 179, 847).

One exemplar of the French translation of Aristotle's *Politics,* completed by Nicholas Oresme for Charles V (A 202) (two also in the king's
own library [484, 485], and two in the library of the duke of Berry [151,
152]; copies were generally available in court libraries).[60] One exemplar of
the commentaries by Albertus Magnus and Peire d'Alvernha on the Latin
translation by William of Moerbecke (active at the papal court in the second
half of the thirteenth century) of the same Aristotelian treatise (A 183).

Two exemplars of the original Latin (A 531, 846) and three of the
French translation (A 232, 240, 243) of *De regimine principum* by Egidio
Romano, dedicated to King Philip (the Fair) of France (no less than eight
copies in the library of Charles V [511–18]). In this treatise Egidio (who
touched upon musical subjects in other of his works as well)[61] took the

56   F. Alberto Gallo, "Die Notationslehre im 14. und 15. Jahrhundert," in *Geschichte der Musiktheorie,* vol. 5 (Darmstadt, 1984), pp. 336–37.

57   Magenta, *I Visconti e gli Sforza,* vol. 1, p. 219.

58   F. Alberto Gallo, "Astronomy and Music in the Middle Ages: The *Liber introductorius* by Michael Scot," *Musica disciplina* 27 (1973): 5–9.

59   F. Alberto Gallo, "Greek Text and Latin Translations of the Aristotelian *Musical Problems:* A Preliminary Account of the Sources," in *Music Theory and Its Sources: Antiquity and the Middle Ages,* ed. André Barbera (Notre Dame, Ind., 1990), pp. 190–96.

60   Lewis Lockwood, *Music in Renaissance Ferrara 1400–1505* (Oxford, 1984), pp. 14, 83–84.

example of Aristotle's *Politics,* asserting that the prince or noble should be instructed in the practice of music. He affirms that

> *musica . . . convenit ipsis iuvenibus et maxime filiis liberorum et nobilium*

music . . . is appropriate for these youths, and especially for the sons of freemen and nobles

adding that

> *ocium bonum est aliquando interponere delectationes musicales que sunt licite et innocue. Maxime autem hoc decens est filiis liberorum et nobilium qui, non vacantes moechanicis artibus, remanerent ociosi nisi studerent liberalibus disciplinis et nisi suis exercitiis interponerent delectationes musicales que sunt licite et honeste.*[62]

a good break [from their studies] is to have them sometimes enjoy music that is permissible and harmless. And this is especially fitting for the sons of freemen and nobles, who, not being free to take up mechanical arts, would be idle when they were not engaged in the liberal disciplines, unless sometimes there could be interspersed with their studies the enjoyment of music that is permissible and wholesome.

But music is not only a pleasant diversion. The prince or noble must

> *illas scientias scire per quas quis se et alios novit regere et gubernare; huismodi autem sunt scientie morales*

know those sciences by means of which one knows how to rule and govern both himself and others; the moral sciences are of this sort,

and at this lordly level a knowledge of music is important,

> *nam et de musica, secundum Philosophum in Politicis, eos scire decet in quantum deservit ad bonos mores.*[63]

for according to the Philosopher in the *Politics,* they ought also to know about music insofar as it is conducive to good character.

The program of education Egidio delineated is divided into three phases. Up to the age of seven, when children begin to understand the meaning

61 F. Alberto Gallo, "Die Musik in der Einteilung der Wissenschaften bei Egidius Romanus und Johannes Dacus," in *Report of the XI Congress of the International Musicological Society* (Copenhagen, 1974), pp. 388–90.

62 Egidius Romanus, *De regimine principum* (Rome, 1607), p. 307.

63 Ibid., p. 310.

of words, they would be told fables and stories, and "aliqui cantus honesti" (some respectable songs) could be sung to them.[64] From ages seven to fourteen, instruction would concern grammar, dialectics, and "practica musicali," consisting of "quadam modulantia vocum" (a certain modulation of voices), probably the singing of solo songs.[65] After age fourteen, when students have fully developed the ability to reason, they would begin the study of the various disciplines while continuing with "practica musica," which would now consist "in consonantia vocum" (in the consonance of voices), possibly a reference to polyphonic song.[66]

III

It was for Verde Visconti (Bernabò's daughter, who married Leopold of Austria in 1365) that perhaps the first abridgement and reelaboration of the *Tacuinum sanitatis* (mentioned above) as a book of illustrations was prepared.[67] All the introductions to the different subjects were eliminated, leaving only the definitions that had originally been presented in the various tables and now were used as legends for the illustrations. Because these illustrations did not belong to the previous, purely textual, tradition of the *Tacuinum,* they constituted a kind of fourteenth-century "translation" of the thirteenth-century Latin text, which itself was a translation of the original Arabic written two centuries earlier. The section on music in this illustrated *Tacuinum* addresses only two of the three divisions in the original treatise, "cantus" and "organ[are c]antum vel pulsare." The first (see fig. 1) is represented by two youths singing under the guidance of a master and in the presence of a royal listener, perhaps David, who symbolized sacred music. For the second category (see fig. 2) there is a scene of three instrumentalists playing respectively a portative organ, a vielle, and a shawm. An isolated illustration for the third division of music, "sonare et balare," appears in another illustrated version of the *Tacuinum;* this volume was the work of Giovannino de Grassi, architect and painter in the

---

64   Ibid., p. 330.
65   Ibid., p. 333.
66   Ibid., p. 337.
67   Paris, Bibliothèque Nationale, MS nouv. acq. latin 1613, fols. 85v–86r; Elena Berti Toesca, *Il "Tacuinum sanitatis" della Biblioteca Nazionale di Parigi* (Bergamo, [1936]).

service of Giangaleazzo, hence it too was produced for the Visconti court.[68] The illustration (fig. 3) presents four female figures, one of them a child (possibly specific individuals at court?), dancing hand in hand to the sounds of a shawm and a bagpipe. In a third, slightly later, illustrated exemplar of the same treatise, also traceable to the Visconti court,[69] the characteristics of all three divisions of music are depicted with much greater precision. "Cantus" (fig. 4) is clearly identified as ecclesiastical chant, performed by two youths and two clerics who read from a music book resting on a lectern. For "organare cantum vel sonare" (fig. 5), here understood as song accompanied by the sound of instruments, we see a singer performing between players on the vielle and the portative organ. Finally, the illustration for "sonare et balare" (fig. 6) refers to court dancing, in this scene of a woman holding hands with a man on either side, all stepping lightly as a shawm and a bagpipe resound in the castle hall. These three illustrations seem to organize the images of music at the Visconti court into a clear, coherent system that was to find its best expression in the artistry of Giovannino de Grassi.

There are two scenes in a collection of Giovannino's work[70] that correspond perfectly to the "cantus" and "organare cantum" in the illustrated versions of the *Tacuinum*. Figure 7 shows five singers, some in ecclesiastical dress, who are singing from a parchment scroll that contains a melody in notation typical of liturgical books, and syllables of text. Figure 8 is of two maidens, one playing the harp (reminiscent perhaps of Valentina Visconti, Senleches, Vannozzo?) while the other sings. A third illustration that would complete the series, for "sonare et saltare," can be found in a small contemporary collection of drawings from the area of Lombardy;[71] here two elegantly dressed couples are dancing to the sound of a lute (fig. 9).

---

68   Liège, Bibliothèque Universitaire, MS 1041, fol. 64v; Luisa Cogliati Arano, *Tacuinum sanitatis* (Milan, 1976, 1979); English translation: Luisa Cogliati Arano, *The Medieval Health Handbook: Tacuinum Sanitatis,* translated and adapted by Oscar Ratti and Adele Westbrook (New York, 1976).

69   Rome, Biblioteca Casanatense, MS 4182, fols. 200, 201, 202; *"Theatrum Sanitatis" di Bubuchasym de Baldach: Cod. 4182 della Biblioteca Casanatense di Roma,* ed. Adalberto Pazzini, Emma Pirani, and Mario Salmi (Parma, 1970).

70   Bergamo, Biblioteca Civica, MS D VII 14, fols. 3v, 5v; Howard Mayer Brown, "Catalogus: A Corpus of Trecento Pictures with Musical Subjects," *Imago musicae* 5 (1988): 194–95.

71   New York, Pierpont Morgan Library, MS II 2, fol. 13r; Brown, "Catalogus," pp. 236–39.

These three images of music were united yet again in the miniatures that Giovannino de Grassi created for Giangaleazzo Visconti's Book of Hours.[72] In this case they embellish the initial letters of three psalms. The use of musical elements in the illustration for Psalm 97 (98), *Cantate Domino* (fig. 10), reflects an iconographic tradition that was particularly popular in France.[73] Here music is represented in a sacred context: a group of eight choristers, consisting of clerics and knights, is singing from an open parchment scroll containing a type of musical notation used in liturgical books, with one syllable of text. Such activity would have been well served by the numerous notated liturgical books that were present in the Visconti library: from a "liber cantus" (book of song) that began with the Christmas offertory (A 51), to the "misse dominicales in cantu" (Sunday Masses in song) (A 60), to a series of Ambrosian antiphonaries (A 61–64), to the "officium corporis Christi scriptum cum cantu" (Office of Corpus Christi, with music) (A 85). Ecclesiastical chant was by no means extraneous to the musical life of the court: on the ground floor of the castle at Pavia, in fact, there was a chapel where Giangaleazzo would attend daily Mass.[74]

The musical elements used for the illustration of Psalm 80 (81), *Exultate Deo* (fig. 11) are again in accordance with iconographic tradition.[75] Besides King David's ever-present psaltery, in the background there are two players with long trumpets, each displaying a banner with the Visconti coat of arms; and in the foreground we see two singers and three instrumentalists who are playing respectively a pair of small drums (Francesco di Vannozzo dedicated one of his sonnets to this instrument as well: "Tamburlo mio, sarestu mai quel messo" [O drum of mine, would ever you be that messenger]),[76] a portative organ, and a vielle. This group could be

---

72 Florence, Biblioteca Nazionale Centrale, MS Banco Rari 397, fols. 90v, 76v, 120v; *The Visconti Hours: National Library, Florence,* ed. Millard Meiss and Edith W. Kirsch (New York, 1972).

73 Genette Foster, "The Iconology of Musical Instruments and Musical Performance in Thirteenth-Century French Manuscript Illuminations" (Ph.D. dissertation, City University of New York, 1977; available in photocopy or film from University Microfilms, Ann Arbor), pp. 32–39.

74 Magenta, *I Visconti e gli Sforza.*

75 Foster, "Iconology," pp. 14–15, 27–28.

76 Medin, *Le rime di Francesco di Vannozzo,* pp. 166–67.

performing a polyphonic piece, since music here has to do with the sounds of festivities and ceremonial celebrations.

Whereas the texts of the two preceding psalms contain references to music, the musical features in the illustration for Psalm 121 (122), *Letatus sum* (fig. 12), have no correlation with the text, nor do they follow any kind of iconographic tradition. Instead of the traditional King David playing his psaltery, here we see a young prince entirely resembling the portraits of Giangaleazzo that decorate other pages of this Book of Hours as a sign of his patronage.[77] Temperance and Strength on the left side of the scene allude to the "Count of Virtue," while the crown is a telling indication of the regal ambitions entertained by a man who aspired to become lord over all of Italy (Antonello da Caserta's madrigal celebrating the investiture of Giangaleazzo as duke speaks of the "novo Re" [new king][78]). At the feet of the "king" are two hounds, a Visconti passion since the days of the musical caccia. He plays no instrument but listens to the psaltery, vielle, and portative organ. It seems to be the sound of chamber music, probably dance music, a private entertainment like the game of chess being played by the canopied couple in the lower right corner. "Letatus sum," begins the psalm, which sings of the joy of the believer before the walls of Jerusalem; but this scene illustrates instead the joys to be found within the walls of a castle, with music as a central element in the representation of perfect happiness.

77   Edith W. Kirsch, *Five Illuminated Manuscripts of Giangaleazzo Visconti* (London, 1991), pp. 39–67.
78   *Lucca Codex*, p. 38.

FIGURE 1 Paris, Bibliothèque Nationale, MS nouv. acq. latin 1613, *Tacuinum sanitatis,* fol. 85v.

CANTUS

SINGING

Legend, obscure here, seems nearly identical to that of figure 4.

Cantus.

Nature scordart noces istrumetozum ... lit certus.
neltoz erces qui aliat ... Inuamentri. ...
twombus nocumetum ... aluebsli ... pter ...
remono noi. a ... quil ... tui.

FIGURE 2   Paris, Bibliothèque Nationale, MS nouv. acq. latin. 1613, *Tacuinum sanitatis,* fol. 86r.

ORGAN[ARE C]ANTUM VEL PULSARE

Nature. quedam in vita vel cantus molentus. melius exeo. quod est proportionatum concorditer cum voce. Iuvamentum quando cantat suaviter non festinanter. nocumentum quando discorditer cantatur quando ipsorum. alterum vix audietur oculte cantare. remotio nocumenti. cum proportionaliter concordatur.

ACCOMPANYING A SONG OR PLAYING MUSIC

Nature: a certain pleasantness in life or in singing. *The better [sort] of it* [shortened hereafter to "better"]: that which is in agreeable relationship with the voice. *Usefulness:* when one sings sweetly and not hurriedly. *Harmfulness:* when something is sung discordantly; when one can hardly hear what another softly sings. *Removal of harm:* when the singing together is well-balanced.

Organariu ul' pulsare.

latur quedā in uita ul' cātr̄ molentꝰ meluis exeo. q̄ est ꝑ
pꝛtionati concorditer ai uoce. luuamentū qn cantat suauit
non festinanter. nocumentūqn discorditer cantat qd ipꝛu̅.
alterii uix audietur oculte cantare. icinono noci. ai ꝓꝑtioꝰa
liter ꝫcoꝛdatur.

FIGURE 3 Liège, Bibliothèque Universitaire, MS 1041, *Tacuinum sanitatis,* fol. 64v. Illustration by Giovannino de Grassi.

SONARE ET BALARE

Nature. movere pedes et persona et proportionaliter ad sonum melius ex eo quando proportionaliter intibi ciosono [sic; compare figure 6] et actus persone. Iuvamentum participatio videndi et audiendi in delectatione et consonatie nocumentum est receditur aconsonantia notarum Remotio nocumenti. reditur notarum consonantia

PLAYING MUSIC AND DANCING

Nature: moving the feet and the person to music. *Better:* when the [intention of the music] and the action of the person are matching. *Usefulness:* participating in watching and listening in delight and consonance. *Harmfulness* is when it departs from the consonance of the notes. *Removal of harm:* the consonance of notes is restored.

Sonare et balare.

Nature . mouere sexes et psonā et p porcionalitē ao soni
melius et eo quāto p porcionalit̄ i tibi aosono et actus
psone. J iuuamētū p tiapatio verdi et auoiendi in oe
lectaticē et consonatie nocimūtū est retedir 4 sonātia notar
Remouo nocumēti . reoit notar consonātia

FIGURE 4 Rome, Biblioteca Casanatense, MS 4182, *Theatrum sanitatis,* fol. 200.

CANTUS

Nature. Concordari voces instrumentoru*m* q*uando* necesarie su*nt* usus. melius ex eo. qui alicit a*nimo*s. Iuvame*ntum* liberat ab egritudinib*us*. nocume*ntum*. q*uando* asuescu*nt* p*ropter* delectatione*m*. remot*io* nocum*ent*i. cu*m* utu*n*tur p*ropter* iuvame*ntum* cantus.

SINGING

Nature: the concord of voices and of instruments, when it is necessary to use them. *Better:* that which draws the soul to it. *Usefulness:* it frees one from sufferings. *Harmfulness:* when they become accustomed to it for the sake of pleasure. *Removal of harmfulness:* when they use it for the benefits of singing.

Nature. Concordan noces instrumentoriy qn necciane fiit usus. melius
ex co. qui aliat aios. Juvamétiz, liberat ab egritroinib, nocumétiz, qn asue
scit ꝑ delectarione; remoto nocum. cu utitur ꝑ iuvamétu cantus.

FIGURE 5 Rome, Biblioteca Casanatense, MS 4182, *Theatrum sanitatis,* fol. 201.

ORGANARE CANTUM VEL SONARE

Nature. Quedam in vita vel cantus molentus. melior ex eis quando est proportionatus concorditer cum voce. Iuvamentum. quando cantant suaviter et non festinant. nocumentum. quando discorditer cantant quando ipsorum alterum vix audietur oculte cantare. remotio nocumenti cum proportionaliter concordantur.

ACCOMPANYING A SONG OR PLAYING MUSIC

Nature: a certain pleasantness in life or in singing. *Better:* when it is in agreeable relationship with the voice. *Usefulness:* when they sing sweetly and they do not hurry. *Harmfulness:* when they sing discordantly; when one can hardly hear what another softly sings. *Removal of harm:* when the singing together is well-balanced.

Natiur. Quedam in uita uel cantus molentius melioz ex eis. qo est ppoz
tionatus xorditer cā uoce Juuamētū. qn cantant suauiter qno festinat.
noccumētū. qn discorditer cantant qr ipoz alter aur audietur occulte canti
re remoto noccumti ei apportionaliter xordantur.

FIGURE 6 Rome, Biblioteca Casanatense, MS 4182, *Theatrum sanitatis,* fol. 202. Notice the addition, written in above the first line, of the missing first phrase (compare figure 3).

SONARE ET BALARE

Nature. quando *proporcionaliter* adequat intentio soni *et* actus persone. Iuvame*ntum*. participatio videndi in delectat[*ione*] *con*sonantie. nocume*ntum*. cu*m* recedu*nt* aconsona*ntia* notaru*m*. remot*io* nocume*n*-ti. cu*m* reddit*ur* ad*consonantia*m nota*rum*.

PLAYING MUSIC AND DANCING

Nature: {moving the feet and the person to music. *Better:*} when the intention of the music and the action of the person are matching and equal. *Usefulness:* participating in watching, in the delightfulness of the consonance. *Harmfulness:* when they depart from the consonance of the notes. *Removal of harm:* when it is restored to the consonance of the notes.

Sonare et balare

mouet prdes exysonia pspornonali adf isu k a'ut

Natine, quatroo, sporcionalir ad equar uitentiosomi ⁊ actus perione. Ju
uamentis, partiapatio uitendoi un delectatoe osonantie ncaumentis. cu re
cediir aconsonatia notaru, retmoto ncaumnt, cu recthr ado sonatia notag.

FIGURE 7 Bergamo, Biblioteca Civica, MS D VII 14, fol. 3v.

Singing: illustration from a collection of works by Giovannino de Grassi.

FIGURE 9 New York, Pierpont Morgan Library, MS II 2, fol. 13r.

Playing music and dancing: illustration from a collection of four-teenth-century drawings from Lombardy.

FIGURE 10 Florence, Biblioteca Nazionale Centrale, MS Banco Rari 397, *The Visconti Book of Hours,* fol. 90v. Miniature by Giovannino de Grassi.

Beginning of Psalm 97 (98): Cantate domino canticum novum. quia mirabilia fecit. Salvavit sibi dexteram eius. et brachium sanctum eius. Notum fecit . . .

domino canticum nouum . quia mirabilia
fecit . **S**aluauit sibi dexteram eius . et
brachium sanctum eius **N**otum fecit

FIGURE 11 Florence, Biblioteca Nazionale Centrale, MS Banco Rari 397, *The Visconti Book of Hours,* fol. 76v. Miniature by Giovannino de Grassi.

Beginning of Psalm 80 (81): Exultate deo adiutori nostro. iubilate deo iacob. Sumite psalmum et date tympanum. psalterium iocundum cum cythara. Bucinate ineomenia tuba. ininsigni diei sollempni ˙ . . .

adiutori nostro. iubilate deo iacob. Su=
mite psalmum et date tympanum. psaltei
um iocundum cum cythara. Buccinate
in comenia tuba. in insigni diei sollempni

FIGURE 12 Florence, Biblioteca Nazionale Centrale, MS Banco Rari 397, *The Visconti Book of Hours,* fol. 120v. Miniature by Giovannino de Grassi.

Beginning of Psalm 121 (122): Letatus sum . . .

Above this is the end of Psalm 120 (121): . . . q*ue* luna per noctem Dominus custodit te ab omni malo. custodiat animam tua*m* dominus. Dominus custodiat introytum tuum. et exitum tuum. exhoc nunc *et* usq*ue* inseculum.

Rubric: Feria iii. ad vesperum. Psalmus david. (Wednesday at Vespers; a psalm of David.)

quc

Three

"ORPHEUS
CHRISTIANUS"

Between May and October 1473 Ludovico Carboni, orator in the service of Ercole d'Este and teacher of rhetoric at the University of Ferrara, wrote his *Dialogus de neapolitana profectione.*[1] Dedicated to Ferdinand of Aragon, king of Naples, the work describes how a delegation of the Este family had traveled to Naples to meet Leonora, Ferdinand's daughter and Ercole d'Este's betrothed, and accompany her back to Ferrara. Carboni was part of this group, and he delivered the official oration in Naples. The dialogue supposedly takes place during festivities the royal court organized in honor of the guests from Ferrara and in celebration of Leonora's departure. One of the speakers, a Neapolitan by the name of Paolo Marchesi, is weary of all the various organized entertainments, the balls and dances, the joustings and tournaments; Carboni, on the other hand, would gladly go on, but he acquiesces to friends who wish to hear the tale of his trip from Ferrara to Naples. However, he proposes to preface the prose narration with a brief summary in verse (twenty-one hexameters) and therefore says to Marchesi:

> *vocandus est cum lyra sua Franciscus tuus, nec enim sine cantu aliquo proferenda sunt carmina, et ex nimia lassitudine vox mea rauca facta est.*

---

1 *Ludovici Carbonis Dialogus de neapolitana profectione*, Vatican City, Biblioteca Apostolica Vaticana, MS vaticano latino 8618, fols. 32r–79r. Cf. Isabella Nuovo, "Sulla struttura di un dialogo di Ludovico Carbone," *Annali della Facoltà di Lettere e Filosofia, Università degli Studi di Bari* 21 (1978): 93–112.

> your Francesco should be called with his *lyra,* for verses should not be
> presented without any singing, and my voice is hoarse from extreme
> fatigue.

When not impeded by this occasional hoarseness, Ludovico Carboni
would sing and accompany his Latin compositions himself, as he states in
one of his orations:

> *Ego certe versus meos ut plurimum facio apolleneam cytharam in manu tenens.*[2]
>
> Indeed I perform my verses as I usually do, with my Apollonian
> cithara in my hands.

One of his colleagues in Ferrara, Raffaele Zovenzoni, had even compared
him to the mythical musician Amphion:

> *Candide hinc Carbo, labris Amphionis unus*
> *allectans quercus flumina saxa feras.*[3]
>
> Therefore, fair Carboni, one who has the lips of Amphion,
> charming trees, rivers, rocks, and wild beasts.

His improvisational ability is also documented in several surviving "extem-
porarii versus."[4]

Carboni's practice of singing Latin verses and accompanying himself
on a stringed instrument was perhaps the result of his having studied with
Guarino Veronese in Ferrara. Guarino does not seem ever to have been
personally and directly concerned with music, but his reading of the
ancient writers must certainly have brought him to understand its importance. As early as 1408, in a letter to Francesco Barbaro[5] (to whom he
would later give an important Greek codex on music theory),[6] he had
commented at length on the figure of Timotheus, court musician to
Alexander the Great, who could use his art to inspire a variety of emo-
tional responses in the king: "adeo . . . musicos potuisse concentus fama
est" (so great, it is said, was the power of his harmonious music). In a let-

---

2 Bologna, Biblioteca Universitaria, MS 2948, t. 23, p. 371.

3 Remigio Sabbadini, *Raffaele Zovenzoni e la sua "Monodia Chrysolorae"* (Catania, 1899).

4 Vatican City, Biblioteca Apostolica Vaticana, MS ottoboniano latino 1153, fol. 181.

5 *Epistolario di Guarino Veronese,* ed. Remigio Sabbadini, vol. 1 (Venice, 1915), p. 8.

6 Aubrey Diller, "The Library of Francesco and Ermolao Barbaro," *Italia medievale e umanistica* 6 (1963): 258.

ter to Vitaliano Faella in 1424,[7] Guarino tells of having participated in a banquet enlivened by the presence of musicians

> *qui arte atque harmonia ita sensus deliniebant, ut ex Timothei schola exisse apparerent.*

> who so developed the meaning with their skill and harmonious music, that they appeared to have come from the school of Timotheus.

And he continues with a reminder:

> *maiores nostri non lascivientem, sed sobriam conviviis adhibere musicam; quocirca nullas fere festas apud prius saeculum legis, quibus cantores non interfuissent.*

> our ancestors had not lascivious but serious music at their banquets; you read about hardly any feasts of ancient times in which singers were not involved.

Among the singers he mentions are Iopas at the court of Dido, and Ulysses at the court of Alcinous. How much these thoughts influenced Guarino's pedagogy is suggested by Carboni in the famous funeral oration he wrote for his departed teacher.[8] Several times he mentions the extraordinary fascination of Guarino's voice:

> *Currebatur undique ad vocem iucundissimam*

> People flocked from all directions to his most pleasing voice

and the "musicality" of his readings:

> *Adhuc insonare videtur in auribus meis vox illa dulcissima, sive M. Tullium sive Maronem sive Iuvenalem sive alium quempiam vel oratorem vel poetam vel historicum sive latinum sive graecum legeret.*

> That sweet, sweet voice still seems to sound in my ears, reading maybe Cicero or Virgil or Juvenal or some other orator or poet or historian, either Latin or Greek.

In one of the epitaphs inserted within the same oration, Carboni explicitly credits Guarino with teaching his students to compose Latin verses with musical accompaniment:

---

7 *Epistolario di Guarino,* 1: 405.

8 *Prosatori latini del Quattrocento,* ed. Eugenio Garin (Milan and Naples, 1952), p. 392.

Texere perdocui resonanti carmina plectro.[9]

I taught [them] well how to weave verses with sounding plectrum.

The theoretical foundation for this practice among nobles and men of letters educated in the Guarinian manner was a treatise entitled *De ingenuis moribus et liberalibus studiis adolescentie,* written by Pierpaolo Vergerio in 1402 for Ubertino, son of Francesco da Carrara, lord of Padua. When Guarino first acquired a copy of this treatise in 1429, his friends frequently asked to borrow it: "multi a me illud petunt vel efflagitant magis" (many asked me for it, or rather demanded it).[10] As a student in Ferrara, Leonello d'Este later gave his teacher another beautiful copy of the work. Guarino marked this copy with the names of its proprietor and provenance—

> *Hoc libello me Guarinum Veronensem donavit Illustr. Leonellus Estensis.*[11]

> The illustrious Leonello d'Este presented me, Guarino Veronese, with this book.

He also used it for a course of university lessons, of which we still have the inaugural address:

> *Oratiuncula Guarini Veronensis oratoris clarissimi pro libello* De ingenuis moribus *inchoando.*[12]

> Brief oration of the great orator Guarino Veronese, to introduce the book *De ingenuis moribus.*

In this "praeclarissimo libello" (most splendid book), as Guarino called it, Vergerio—drawing on the teachings in the eighth book of Aristotle's *Politics*—includes music among the four essential disciplines (along with grammar, gymnastics, and drawing) in the education of a young noble. He specifically recommends the practice of singing accompanied by an instrument:

> *Sed ne erit quidem indecens cantu fidibusque laxare animum.*

> But it certainly will not be inappropriate for them to relax with song and stringed instruments.

---

9   Ibid., p. 410.
10   *Epistolario di Guarino,* vol. 2 (1916), p. 85.
11   Modena, Biblioteca Estense, MS a M 9 8.
12   Ferrara, Biblioteca Ariostea, MS II. 110, fols. 112v–113r.

The precedent for this practice was to be found in no less distinguished an example than Homer's Achilles:

Achillem Homerus inducit a pugna redeuntem in hac re solitum acquiescere.[13]

Homer presents Achilles as accustomed to rest in this manner when returning home from battle.

Guarino's students were taught to aspire to this ideal. The most illustrious of them, Leonello d'Este, received a letter from his teacher (ca. 1434) regarding the usefulness of musical activity, wherein Guarino cited the example of Achilles just as Vergerio had done:

Quid Achillem Graecorum fortissimum? num post martios sudores citharam tractasse cantuque animos laxasse ab Homero traditum est?[14]

What about Achilles, the bravest of the Greeks? What about Homer telling us that after the sweat of battle, he took up his cithara and relaxed with song?

Leonello's reassuring response is intentionally styled in similar terms:

Cantui et fidibus laxandi animi gratia temporis quicquam concedo.[15]

I allow myself some time for relaxing by singing and playing music.

Even if we disregard the various declarations of interest in, or even passion for, music that were made by other Guarino students, from Leonardo Giustinian[16] to Giorgio Valagussa,[17] the diffusion of accompanied song in university circles at Ferrara is amply documented by Ludovico Carboni himself, who, in several of his orations, mentions specific individuals. One was the rector of students at the University of Ferrara, "Rainaldus" (most probably Rainaldus de Guarneriis, who held that position in the period 1458–60):[18]

---

13 "*Petri Pauli Vergerii ad Ubertinum de Carraria de ingenuis moribus et liberalibus adolescentiae studiis liber,*" ed. Carlo Miani, in *Atti e memorie della Società Istriana di Archeologia e Storia Patria,* Nuova serie 20–21 (1972–73): 183–251.

14 *Epistolario di Guarino,* 2: 275.

15 Ibid., p. 277.

16 Ibid., p. 296.

17 Gianvito Resta, *Giorgio Valagussa, umanista del Quattrocento* (Padua, 1964), pp. 133–34, 245.

18 Giuseppe Pardi, *Lo Studio di Ferrara nei secoli XV e XVI* (Ferrara, 1903), p. 71.

Si quando laxandi animi gratia concessam aliquam hilaritatem peteret, lyram sumebat in manus et continuo labore defessos spiritus dulcis harmonia recreabat.[19]

If sometimes he would seek some enjoyment, which he would allow himself for the sake of relaxation, he would take up his *lyra* in his hands and with sweet harmony refresh his spirit, worn out with continual labor.

Another was a Ferrarese youth whose description again includes a closing reference to Achilles:

Quod si ei detur otii, non in voluptatibus, sed in rebus laude dignis consumere consuevit: musica, enim, et fidibus incredibiliter delectatur . . . non tamen viro docto indignum iudicabitur sumere aliquando lyram et relaxare animum gravissimis curis fessum atque ad aliquam concessam hilaritatem revocare. Nam et Homerus Achillem a pugna redeuntem virorum fortium laudes modulantem inducit.[20]

If he had any leisure time, he was accustomed to spend it, not in sensual indulgence, but in praiseworthy activities: for he took incredible delight in music and playing a stringed instrument . . . for it will not be judged unworthy of a learned man to sometimes take up the *lyra*, to relax his spirit worn out with very serious cares, and to let himself have some fun. For Homer presents Achilles returning from battle singing the praises of brave men.

The presence of a stringed instrument in the court library of the Este castle at Ferrara is further, physical evidence that such musical practice was part of this cultural context. As Angelo Decembrio wrote:

intra bibliothecam insuper . . . citharamque habere non dedecet: si ea quandoque delecteris.[21]

in the library also . . . it is not unbecoming to have a cithara, if you might sometimes enjoy it.

Certainly the ancient practice of improvising verses in song with instrumental accompaniment was particularly fashionable at Ferrara; but its popularity was not limited to that court alone. Ludovico Carboni no doubt met one of the most famous improvisors in Naples during his stay

---

19   Vatican City, Biblioteca Apostolica Vaticana, MS ottoboniano latino 1153, fol. 189r.
20   Ibid., fol. 115r.
21   Angelo Decembrio, *Politia litteraria* (Augsburg, 1540), p. 3.

there in 1473: this was Aurelio Brandolini, also called Lippo (rheum-eyed) because of his severe visual handicap.[22] Born in Florence in 1454, Brandolini had moved to Naples at an early age, and with the patronage of King Ferdinand he was able to complete his studies there. According to his brother Raffaele (also a poet and musician, and the author of a small treatise in praise of music and poetry), Aurelio's ability to improvise earned him the admiration of many important members of the Neapolitan court:

> *tantumque assiduitate et commendatione Neapoli perfecit, ut dum apud Ferdinandum primum Neapolitanorum regem, apud Antonellum Petrutium intimum illius regis a secretis ministrum, apud Julium Aquavivum excellentissimum comitem ac Andream Matheum filium marchionem, apud plerosque regni proceres summo et animo et ingenio adornatos, heroicas laudes extemporali carmine celebraret, plurimum et laudis et gratiae reportavit.*[23]

> by his unremitting application and excellent recommendation, he accomplished so much in Naples that he gained great praise and favor when he celebrated heroic praises in extemporaneous verse, before Ferdinand, the first king of Naples; before Antonello Petrucci, the king's privy minister; before the most excellent count Giulio Aquaviva and his son Andrea Matteo, the marquis; and before many nobles of the realm endowed with the ultimate in character and talent.

The learned Antonello Petrucci was secretary to King Ferdinand and maintained a library of great renown, while the Aquaviva d'Atri family were major exponents of Neapolitan nobility and culture. Andrea Matteo in particular must have been interested in music, since he published a Latin translation of Plutarch's *De virtute morali* complete with an extensive commentary that includes matters of music theory.[24] The first book of this commentary closes with an anecdote on the power of music and the passion that King Ferdinand himself had for accompanied song. It tells of an individual who had lost the king's favor but was able to redeem himself in this way:

22   Enrico Mayer, "Un umanista italiano della corte di Mattia Corvino: Aurelio Brandolini Lippo," *Studi e documenti italo-ungheresi della R. Accademia d'Ungheria di Roma*, 2 (1938): 120–68.

23   Raffaele Brandolini, *De musica et poetica opusculum*, Rome, Biblioteca Casanatense, MS 805, fol. 85.

24   Francesco Tateo, *Chierici e feudatari del Mezzogiorno* (Bari, 1984), pp. 76–84.

accepta cithara, cantilenam qua rex maxime delectatur, sub fenestra regis
cecinit.[25]

he took up his cithara and beneath the window of the king he sang a
song which delighted the king greatly.

Listening to musicians as they sing and play stringed instruments was
recommended by the authoritative Giovanni Pontano in *De principe,* a
book dedicated to Ferdinand of Aragon and destined for the education of
his son Alfonso:

Adhibendi sunt etiam musici qui tum cantu tum chordis oblectent animum et
curas permulceant.[26]

Musicians also should be brought in, to cheer the soul and soothe
away cares with song and stringed instruments.

Another contribution to Alfonso's education was an Italian translation of
Egidio Romano's *De regimine principum,*[27] with its Aristotelian emphasis on
the importance of musical study.[28]

Little remains of the improvised and sung poetry Brandolini produced during his Neapolitan period (apart from the verses collected in
the booklet *De laudibus musicae et Petriboni ferrariensis,* which will be discussed below). Perhaps he is author of the verses in praise of Federico da
Montefeltro,[29] thirty-two distichs that begin

Accipe qui fervidus tibi dat, Federice, salutem

Accept, O Federico, one who gives you hearty greetings

and include the author's declaration that he is in the service of the king of
Naples:

Non ego cum sumptu Ferdinandi et munere vivam.

Not I, since I live at the expense and by the gift of Ferdinand.

---

25   Andrea Matteo Acquaviva d'Aragona, *Commentarius in Plutarchi de virtute morali*
(Naples, 1526), fol. 59r.

26   *Ioannis Ioviani Pontani Opera* (Naples, 1512).

27   Rodolfo Renier, "Opere inesplorate di De Gennaro," *Giornale storico della letteratura*
italiana 11 (1888): 469–75.

28   See chapter 2.

29   Adolfo Cinquini, "Spigolature da codici manoscritti del secolo XV: Il codice vaticano
urbinate latino 1193," *Classici e neolatini* 6 (1910): 26–28.

The occasion of these verses might have been Federico's visit to Naples in 1474 to receive the Order of the Ermine, bestowed upon him by Ferdinand.

Brandolini might also have been responsible for some verses sent to Lorenzo de' Medici, which include a commemoration of Lorenzo's own ability to improvise and sing verses:

> *Laurentius ex tempore versus componit et ad lyram canit.*[30]

> Lorenzo composes verses ex tempore and sings to the accompaniment of the *lyra.*

Apollo personally infuses Lorenzo with his art and sings with him:

> *Nunc et uterque simul nocteque dieque moratur*
> *et canit ad doctam doctus uterque lyram.*[31]

> Now both day and night together they tarry
> and each skillful singer sings to skillful accompaniment.

The fact that Brandolini had not, in any case, severed ties with his Florentine origins is demonstrated by the epitaph he wrote in 1480 for the famous organist at the cathedral of Florence, Antonio Squarcialupi. Here Squarcialupi is extolled for having brought the ancient song of the Muses to the sacred music of his day:

> *Musarum arcanos phoebaeo e vertice cantus*
> *decuxi, atque ipsas in nova templa deas.*[32]

> I have brought the secret songs of the Muses down from Apollo's peak,
> and have led the goddesses themselves to new temples.

Meanwhile, in 1479 Aurelio had moved to the papal court in Rome (after giving the academic inaugural oration at Capua, which will be discussed below). Here too the practice of accompanied song had been much admired since the period of Pius II, who (according to Raffaele Brandolini) greatly enjoyed not only hearing but sometimes also playing this genre of music:

---

30 Gino Bottiglioni, *La lirica latina in Firenze nella seconda metà del secolo XV* (Pisa, 1913), pp. 104–11.

31 *Carmina illustrium poetarum italorum*, vol. 2 (Florence, 1719), pp. 439–53.

32 Angelo Maria Bandini, *Bibliotheca Leopoldina Laurentiana seu catalogus manuscriptorum qui nuper in Laurentianam traditi sunt*, vol. 3 (Florence, 1793), p. 250b.

*Pius II pontifex maximus usque adeo poeticis numeris ad lyram est delectatus,
ut unum hoc voluptatis genus caeteris omnibus anteferret, lyramque non solum
libenter audire sed iucundissime interim attingere non gravaretur.*[33]

Pope Pius II took such delight in metrical poetry performed to the
lyra that he valued this one kind of pleasure above all others; he not
only gladly listened to the *lyra,* but he was not unwilling sometimes to
play it himself, and very pleasantly.

Sixtus IV greatly enjoyed Brandolini's poetic and musical ability in numerous private performances dealing with the most varied topics:

*cecinit et tam saepe et tam familiariter et tam diverse apud pontificem ipsum,
ut quotidie in intimo cubicolo nunc pontificias laudes, modo gravissimas
philosophiae quaestiones, nonnumquam sacras historias, variato carmine
enarraret.*[34]

he sang for the pope himself so often and so familiarly and with such
diversity, that daily in his privy chambers he recounted sometimes the
pope's praises, sometimes the most serious philosophical questions,
sometimes sacred history, with a variety of songs.

These "pontificias laudes" can be identified as a group of texts in
hexameters,[35] whose composition was begun "in agro neapolitano" (in the
territory of Naples) and completed during Brandolini's sojourn in Rome
"in ipsa pontificis domo" (in the papal residence itself).[36]

Brandolini remained in Rome during the subsequent pontificate of Inno-
cent VIII. One of his "concerts," which was "recorded" in this period, survives
in a copy made by the Venetian chronicler Marin Sanudo.[37] The performance
probably dates from 1485[38] and took place before a group of Venetian patri-
cians. Bernardo Bembo, orator of Venice at the papal court, was among them,
as was his son Pietro, the future man of letters then fifteen years old, who

---

33   R. Brandolini, *De musica et poetica,* fol. 16v.

34   Ibid., fol. 85v.

35   Eugène Müntz, *Les arts à la cour des Papes pendant le XVe et le XVIe siècle* (Paris, 1882),
pp. 56–60.

36   Giuseppe de Luca, "Un umanista fiorentino e la Roma rinnovata da Sisto IV," *La
rinascita* 1 (1938): 74–90.

37   Venice, Biblioteca Nazionale Marciana, MS latino XII 210 (=4689). Cf. Vittorio Cian,
"Per Bernardo Bembo: Le relazioni letterarie, i codici e gli scritti," *Giornale storico della letteratura italiana* 31 (1898): 79–80.

38   Nella Giannetto, *Bernardo Bembo, umanista e politico veneziano* (Florence, 1985), pp.
176–77.

transcribed the texts as they were delivered. The first piece is a composition of eight Sapphic strophes, in which Brandolini invokes the Virgin's blessing on the Venetian guests and prays for healing for the pope, who was then ill:

Alma quae caelo residens sereno

. . .

Audias nostras modulante voces
carmina plectro.

Bountiful [Mother] residing in serene heaven,

. . .

Hear our voices as our instruments
make melodious song.

Bernardo Bembo then proposes a theme: "uti tempora deploraret nostra, prisca autem laudaret" (let him deplore our age, but praise antiquity), which Brandolini immediately develops into forty-nine distichs sung to the *lyra:*

Ad latios veniam prompte nunc carmina versus.

I will come quickly now to [the topic of] Latin verses.

The improvisor is so secure in his skill that he challenges the young transcriber to a race:

ipse para calamum, scriptor amice, tuum.
Non poteris mea verba sequi: velocius ibo,
non poteris nostros scribere versiculos.

ready your pen, friend scribe.
You will not be able to keep up with my words; I will go faster;
you will not be able to write down my verses.

Pietro Bembo accepts the challenge and even sportively assumes the blame for any eventual errors in transcription, noting at the foot of the page:

Si quos invenisti versus minus bonos, id erroris ascribito iis qui Lyppo flo-
rentino caeco canente scriptitarunt.

If you find any verses that are not so good, ascribe that to an error on the part of those who were writing while Lippo the blind Florentine was singing.

In conclusion, yielding to the request made by another member of the audience, Pietro Diedo, to sing improvised verses in Italian, Brandolini performs two strophes of eight lines each that begin:

Non debbo avanti la ricolta andare.

I should not exceed the promise made.

This transition to improvisation in the vernacular, which was unusual for Brandolini, is perhaps an "easy-listening piece" offered to the public at the end of the concert. In fact, Raffaele Brandolini places these two types of improvisation—the loftier one in Latin and the lower one in the vernacular—in distinct contrast to one another, due to their respective social and cultural components:

> *At ob hoc ipsum latinum carmen vernaculo est longe praestantius, quod illus senatorio hoc plebeio ordini accomodatur, a viribus illud hoc a paganis; a Romanis illud hoc a barbaris; a doctis illud ac honestissimo bonarum artium negocio delectatis, ab indoctis hoc turpique ocio dissolutis magnopere commendatur.*[39]

> But for this reason a Latin song is much superior to one in the vernacular: because the former is geared to the senatorial rank, the latter to the plebeian; the one is praised by those with powerful minds, the other by bumpkins; the one by Romans, the other by barbarians; the one by the learned who delight in the respectable business of the fine arts, the other by the unlearned, dissolute in their disreputable idleness.

While in Rome Brandolini also became popular for his oratory[40]—both sacred, like the oration in honor of St. Thomas, dedicated to Cardinal Oliviero Carafa; and forensic, like the oration in defense of the Venetian patrician Leonardo Loredan. The esteem that Brandolini's Roman audiences had for his work as rhetorician, poet, and musician was meaningfully captured in the appellation "Orpheus christianus,"[41] which the learned and austere Cardinal Marco Barbo had often used in his regard.

In 1489 Brandolini left Rome for Hungary and the court of King Matthias Corvinus. There he found two individuals he had already known in Naples: Queen Beatrice, the daughter of Ferdinand of Aragon, and the instrumentalist Pietrobono, whom Brandolini had praised in verse. His dialogue *De humanae vitae conditione et toleranda corporis aegritudine* was

---

39   R. Brandolini, *De musica et poetica,* fol. 76v.

40   John W. O'Malley, *Praise and Blame in Renaissance Rome: Rhetoric, Doctrine, and Reform in the Sacred Orations of the Papal Court, c. 1450–1521* (Durham, N.C., 1979).

41   R. Brandolini, *De musica et poetica,* fol. 85v.

composed in this period and dedicated to the king and queen.[42] Among
the various remedies it proposes for alleviating the suffering of illness, listening to instrumental and vocal music was by no means a casual choice:

> *Quanta est illa quae auribus percipitur cum aut musicorum instrumentorum*
> *aut humanarum vocum mira tum consonancia tum varietate tum etiam*
> *suavitate detinemur?*[43]

> How great is that which is perceived by the ears when we are held fast
> by the marvelous consonance or variety or sweetness of either human
> voices or musical instruments?

Following the death of Matthias, Brandolini returned to his native
Florence and entered an Augustinian order. In 1490–91 he taught oratory
and poetics at the center in Pisa of Florence's *studium generale*.[44] His return
also brought him into renewed contact with Angelo Poliziano, with whom
he had maintained a friendship dating, as a letter states, "ab ineunte
aetate" (from an early age).[45] Actually, Raffaele Brandolini mentions a certain hostility on the part of Poliziano: "acutissimis licet Politiani jaculis
appeteretur" (he was the target of Poliziano's very sharp barbs);[46] but professional rivalry may have been the reason, since Raffaele credits Poliziano
with being one of the major improvisors of his day.[47] Aurelio meanwhile
carried on with his oratorical activity; particularly noteworthy is his sermon in the convent of St. Gall for Holy Thursday of 1491.[48]

However, neither religious habit nor academic dignity prevented him
from continuing to improvise poetry in music. Indeed, one of Brandolini's
most famous performances took place in this last period of his life. The
concert was given in Verona on 8 October 1494, hosted by the podestà

---

42   Charles E. Trinkaus, *In Our Image and Likeness: Humanity and Divinity in Italian
Humanistic Thought* (London, 1970), pp. 294–321.
43   Aurelio Brandolini, "*De humanae vitae conditione et toleranda corporis aegritudine*," ed. J.
Abel, in *Irodalomtörténeti Emlékek* (Budapest) 2 (1890): 64.
44   Armando F. Verde, *Lo Studio fiorentino 1473–1503: Ricerche e documenti*, vol. 2 (Florence, 1973), pp. 450–51.
45   Angelo Maria Bandini, *Catalogus codicum latinorum Bibliothecae Mediceae Laurentianae*,
vol. 3 (Florence, 1776), pp. 536–37.
46   R. Brandolini, *De musica et poetica*, fol. 87r.
47   Ibid., fol. 84.
48   John M. McManamon, "Renaissance Preaching, Theory and Practice: A Holy Thursday Sermon of Aurelio Brandolini," *Viator* 10 (1979): 355–70.

Gerolamo Bernardo. A detailed "program" survives with the transcription of all the poetic texts,[49] this time the work of the Veronese poet Virgilio Zavarise:[50]

> *Ad magnificum et clarissimum dominum Hieronimum Bernardum Veronae pretorem Virgilius Zavarisius veronensis in carmina extemporanea Lippi Aurelij thusci a nativitate caeci nunc heremite augustinensis et predicatoris egregii ad lyram decantata in ipsius pretoris aula viii octobris 1494.*

> To the magnificent and most illustrious Lord Gerolamo Bernardo, podestà of Verona: Virgilio Zavarise of Verona, in extemporaneous songs of Lippo Aurelio of Tuscany, blind from birth, now a member of the Hermits of St. Augustine and an outstanding preacher, sung to the *lyra* in the court of the podestà 8 October 1494.

Brandolini's first piece consists of twelve distichs dedicated to the podestà:

> *Qui nostram rexere urbem, Bernarde, fatemur.*

> You who rule our city, O Bernardo, we acknowledge.

Then come verses by Zavarise, also in honor of the podestà, immediately followed by Brandolini's response:

> *Virgilii Zavari[s]i hendecasyllabum in quo Calliope ipsum alloquitur de iustitia clarissimi domini Bernardi Verone pretoris:*
>> *Adsum Calliope diu vocata . . .*
> *Lippus Aurelius hendecasyllabo Virgilii antescripto suam lyram tangens exorsus est:*
>> *Magnum Virgilium sonat poetam . . .*

> The hendecasyllables of Virgilio Zavarise in which Calliope himself speaks of the justice of the most illustrious lord Bernardo, podestà of Verona:
>> I, Calliope, long invoked, am here . . .
> Lippo Aurelio, touching his *lyra* began [in reply] to the above-written hendecasyllables of Virgilio:
>> He sings of the great poet Virgilio . . .

---

49   Paris, Bibliothèque Nationale, MS latin 8315, fols. 89v–97r.

50   Giambattista C. Giuliari, "Della letteratura veronese al cadere del secolo XV e le sue opere a stampa," *Il propugnatore* 6, no. 1 (1873): 202–3.

In the final lines of this response Brandolini announces the next composition, again in distichs:

> *iam maiora canam lyra sonanti,*
> *iam plectrum capiam meum sonorum.*
> *finito hendecasyllabo subsequentes cecinit elegos:*
> > *Credo ego nunc Phoebum plectrum cytharamque tulisse . . .*

> now I will sing to my sounding *lyra,*
> now I will take my resounding plectrum.
> And when the hendecasyllables ended, he sang the following elegy:
> > I believe now that Phoebus has taken up his plectrum and cithara . . .

Then there is another exchange of hendecasyllables—a metric pattern perhaps preferred by Zavarise, who improvised his verses but apparently did not sing them:

> *Virgilius ad Lippum ex tempore:*
> > *Nullam materiam tibi poeta . . .*
> *Lippus ad Virgilium:*
> > *O possem veteres referre vates . . .*

> Virgilio to Lippo ex tempore:
> > You the poet have no material . . .
> Lippo to Virgilo:
> > O, would that I could bring back the ancient poets . . .

At this point Brandolini begins the longest and most complex piece of the entire performance—a eulogy to the illustrious men of Verona in fifty-one distichs:

> *Lippus viros illustres veronenses et patrie nostre laudes celebrat hortatu Petri Donati:*
> > *Non ego nunc tantum peregrino carmine laudes . . .*

> Lippo celebrates the illustrious men of Verona and sings the praise of
> our country at the urging of Pietro Donato:
> > Now I [will] not [sing] praises with only a wandering song . . .

This is followed by the recitation of a prose piece. Brandolini then presents the last piece of the concert (on a religious subject) and concludes with thanks to his public:

Recitata per Ludovicum Cendratum epistola Pontij Pilati ad Tiberium Cae-
sarem qua se purgare nititur de injusta Salvatoris nostri nece, Lippus in Pila-
tum invehit et demum auditoribus gratias agit:

  Non ego sum fessus, sed vox mihi rauca canenti . . .

After Ludovico Cendrato has recited the letter from Pontius Pilate to
Tiberius Caesar, in which Pilate tries to clear himself of the unjust
murder of Our Savior, Lippo inveighs against Pilate and finally thanks
his audience:

  I am not tired, but my voice is hoarse from singing . . .

Despite this assertion that he no longer has any voice, Brandolini's final
piece consists of no less than forty-two improvised distichs.

  A "review" of this concert also survives, in a letter from Matteo Bosso
to Girolamo Campagnola in Padua.[51] On a previous occasion when Bosso
had praised another improvisor on the "*lyra,*" Pamfilo Sasso, he had also
declared his great admiration for Brandolini's exceptional memory, likening him to Pico della Mirandola and Ermolao Barbaro.[52] His description
of the concert in Verona[53] begins with a panegyric of Brandolini as a
sacred orator and a philosopher:

Audivimus modo Veronae prophentatem ex pulpito Lippum florentinum religio-
sum haeremitani ordinis hominem, . . . Hic in primis sanctas litteras amat
easque commodissime tractat atque dispensat. Hic quicquid philosophiae illius
veteris quae ad nos effluxit a graecis, gravis, plena, expolita et emuncta nostris
nunc in gymnasio nescio quo citio exoleta, sic bene callet, ut de ea quum ali-
quid suscipit, non Burleos, non Paulos Venetos, non Strodos, sed Platonem
quidem, Aristotelem, Theophrastum audire videamur.

At Verona we have just heard in the pulpit the prophet Lippo the
Florentine, a religious of the heremetic order, . . . This man loves the
sacred writings above all, and most skillfully treats of them and promul-
gates them. And this man understood whatever ancient philosophy has
come to us from the Greeks, a philosophy that was serious, full, polished, and of keen discernment when it came to us, and now has
grown to maturity—how fast it has happened!—in our gymnasium. He

---

51 Giovanni Soranzo, *L'umanista canonico regolare lateranense Matteo Bosso di Verona*
(1427–1502): I suoi scritti e il suo epistolario (Padua, 1965).

52 Matteo Bosso, *Familiares et secundae epistolae* (Mantova, 1498), letter 83.

53 Ibid., letter 75.

understood this philosophy so well that when he took up some topic from it we seemed to be hearing not some Burleo, or Paolo Veneto, or Strodo, but, in fact, Plato, or Aristotle, or Theophrastus.

Bosso follows this with praise of Brandolini as a poet and musician who even surpasses those of antiquity:

> *Lyra ut licentius loquar, ei caedit Apollo et Amphion. Claros vero poetas hoc uno et superat, quod quae illi cudebant longa pervigilia atque lucerna, iste extemporaliter format et canit.*

> With regard to the *lyra*—let me speak quite boldly—Apollo and Amphion yield to him. By this one thing he is victorious over the famous poets: that what they hammered out through long nights and by burning the midnight oil, he fashions and sings extemporaneously.

The most impressive part of the concert, according to this "critic," was the longest composition, the piece in celebration of the illustrious men of Verona:

> *Lippus vero noster in coetu multorum civium nobilissimorum litterarum cultorum ipsoque astante praetore, quicquid ei ab iis proponi placuit, porrecta illi lyra in quoscumque statim arctavit et modulatus est numeros. Denique de illustribus quoque priscae gloriae viris quibus patria Verona esset, quaestus ut diceret, Catullum, Cornelium Nepotem, Plinium secundum, civitati dignitatem urbisque splendorem luculentissimo prosecutus est carmine ac splendidissimis pro merito laudibus, nulla intercedente cogitatione vel haesitatione cum mora.*

> In a gathering of many of the most noble citizens, patrons of literature, including the podestà himself, no matter what it pleased them to propose to our Lippo, his *lyra* was handed to him and right away he put together and sang metrical verses on whatever it was. Finally, when asked to speak of famous men of ancient glory whose native land was Verona, he, without any hesitation or taking time to think, described at length Catullus, Cornelius Nepos, Pliny the Younger, the dignity of citizenship, and the splendor of the city, with a very fine song that earned most splendid and well-deserved praise.

Bosso ends by telling Campagnola that if Brandolini should ever come to Padua it would be well worth his trouble to go and hear him. This is particularly significant in light of the fact that Campagnola had a young son who was also blind from birth and a capable improvisor on the "*lyra*," just like the subject of Bosso's letter.

Aurelio Brandolini died of the plague in Rome in 1497. He left to us the memory of a man of culture, above all an effective orator and skillful poet, who also had a solid familiarity with music:

> *vir certe eruditissimus, sed eloquentissimus ac disertissimus imprimis, poetaque consumatissimus atque multarum aliarum disciplinarum, maximeque musicae, sufficienter edoctus.*[54]

> a man certainly very learned, but above all very eloquent and fluent, also a consummate poet, and quite adequately educated in many other disciplines, especially music.

II

One of the first musicians to be praised in poetry was Gioachino Cancellieri, organist at the cathedral of Ferrara.[55] Guarino Veronese, who in a letter written in 1426 had called Cancellieri "alter huius aetatis Orpheus" (a present-day Orpheus), dedicated a composition to him in which the first three of its eleven hexameters develop this comparison with the mythological Orpheus.[56] While Orpheus could move animals and stones with his cithara, Gioachino attracts even the deaf and the dead when his hands touch his keyboard:

> *Orphea quid mirum volucres et saxa ferasque*
> *humanumque genus cithara traxisse canora,*
> *cum tua mellifluos modulans manu utraque cantus*
> *alliciat surdos "defunctaque corpora vita"?*

> What marvel is it that the tuneful cithara of Orpheus
> drew to him birds, stones, wild beasts, and humans too,
> when your instrument, producing mellifluous songs from both your hands,
> attracts the deaf and even lifeless bodies?

Guarino's son and student, Battista, closely followed his father's example in the eulogy he wrote for the musician Pietrobono of Ferrara, at that time in the service of Borso d'Este.[57] The eight distichs[58] seem to refer to

---

54   Giacomo Filippo [Foresti] da Bergamo, *Supplementum supplementi cronicarum* (Venice, 1503), p. 437.

55   Enrico Peverada, *Vita musicale nella Chiesa ferrarese del Quattrocento* (Ferrara, 1991), pp. 31–37, 60–63, 74–76, 79–80.

56   *Epistolario di Guarino*, 1: 562–63.

57   Peverada, *Vita musicale*, pp. 25–26, 97–98.

58   Venice, Biblioteca Nazionale Marciana, MS latino XII 135 (=4100), fol. 54v.

the earliest phase of Pietrobono's career, when he sang and accompanied himself on the lute. Battista's comparison of Pietrobono with Amphion, Arion, Orpheus, and even Apollo, concludes in favor of the contemporary musician:

> *Non qui dirceos struxit testudine muros*
> *dulcibus aequabit te, Bone Petre, modis*
> *nec qui ceruleas curvo delphine per undas*
> *fugit ab attonitis carmine remigibus*
> *nec te qui silvas traxit rhodopeius heros,*
> *ipse nec arguta vincet Apollo lyra.*

> He who built the walls of Thebes with his instrument
> will not match you, Pietrobono, with his sweet music,
> nor he who fled through the blue
> waves on the arching dolphin with sounding oars of song,
> nor the Thracian hero who enticed forests to follow him,
> nor will Apollo himself best you with his silver lyre.

He goes on to praise Pietrobono's "oratorical" ability to match a bright melody with joyous songs, and a languid sound with sad texts:[59]

> *Sive refers letos claro modulamine cantus*
> *sive refers humili carmina moesta sono,*
> *exprimis humanas festino pollice voces*
> *et subigis blandam fundere verba chelym.*

> Whether you present happy songs with a bright tune,
> or sad verses with an abject sound,
> you produce human voices with your swift thumb,
> and make your sweet instrument bring forth words.

An analogous structure occurs in the eulogy for Pietrobono by the Bolognese orator Filippo Beroaldo, perhaps written in 1473 when the Este delegation from Ferrara (which included Pietrobono) passed through Bologna on its way to Naples. Of its ten distichs,[60] the first four claim that all of ancient music must be considered inferior now, after which we are introduced to the greatest musician of all:

---

59   F. Alberto Gallo, "Pronuntiatio: Ricerche sulla storia di un termine retorico-musicale," *Acta musicologica* 35 (1963): 38–46.

60   Filippo Beroaldo, *Orationes et quamplures apendiculae versuum* (Bologna, 1491).

En cytharedus adest aevi nova gloria nostri,
Petrus, cognomen ex Bonitate trahens.
Hic celeri dulces percurrit pollice nervos
et movet artifici mobilitate manus.

Behold here is the citharist who is the new glory of our age:
Pietro, whose surname comes from "Goodness" [Bonitas].
He runs along the sweet strings with swift finger
and moves his hand with skillful mobility.

These lines evidently refer to that period of Pietrobono's career in which he dedicated himself largely to instrumental performance. The listener's attention was captivated by his agile hands and fingers:

Exprimit hic fidibus resonantia verba canoris,
est testudo loquax huius in arbitrio.
Perstringunt acies oculorum et lumina fallunt
Petri docta manus articulique leves.

From the singing strings he produces resounding words;
his instrument speaks at his whim.
Pietro's skillful hand and nimble fingers
dazzle the eye and deceive sight.

Still other verses in praise of Pietrobono were composed, probably only shortly thereafter, by Paolo Emilio Boccabella, a Roman man of letters who after 1474 was in the service of Cardinal Francesco Gonzaga, papal legate to Bologna (Gonzaga, who is cited in the last of these nine distichs, was himself an admirer of Pietrobono as well). Here again the ability of the instrumentalist is described as much greater than the fabled prowess of Orpheus and Amphion:[61]

Nunc tamen antiquae superat mendacia famae
ortus ab Eridani naiade Petrus eques.
Dulcius hic ipso cum tendat Apolline cordas
auditor totis sensibus esse velim,
tam varium, tam bene concordat in unum,
tam celerem fidibus exagitatam manum.

61   Weimar, Landesbibliothek, MS Q 114, fols. 33v–34r.

> Now, however, the knight Pietro, born of a naiad of Eridanus [the
>   River Po],
> is triumphant over the lies of ancient fame.
> When he touches his strings more sweetly than Apollo himself,
> I would wish to be his audience with all my senses:
> how varied [his performance], how well it goes together into one,
> how swift his hand, in constant movement on his instrument.

Tribute to Pietrobono also appeared in art and oratory. Two examples
date from 1456: a medal with his portrait and the motto "Orpheum superans" (triumphant over Orpheus), struck by Giovanni Boldù;[62] and the
description of a public performance by the musician, included in the oration that Ludovico Carboni gave in Ferrara when he received his doctor-
ate.[63] The performance was part of a religious ceremonial procession in
which Pietrobono participated on his instrument, followed by an admiring
crowd of all sorts of people, young and old, learned and ignorant:

> *Vidimus paucis ante diebus cum urbem solemni sacerdotum pompa lustraremus,*
> *nostrum illum Peribonium musicum admirabilem lyra psallendo inflammari*
> *quasi divino numine afflatum, quia eum turba magna sequebatur non puero-*
> *rum modo et imperitorum, sed gravium quoque hominum et doctorum.*

> A few days ago, when we were taking part in a solemn procession of
> priests around the city, we saw our admirable musician Pietrobono
> playing his *lyra,* afire like one inspired by a divine power, for a great
> crowd was following him, not only of youngsters and the ignorant, but
> also of venerable and learned men.

The narration provides a striking description of the performer's excite-
ment at his own success and the crowd's unrestrained adulation:

> *gaudebat non mediocriter, gestiebat, laetitiam suam capere non poterat, se*
> *ipsum superare conabatur cum videret neminem ad Christum aspicere, sed in*
> *eum omnes conversos, in eius obtutu defixos mirari tam inauditas modulorum*
> *illecebras quae cuique animum eripiebat, omnes se protesi conculcari, prosterni*
> *aequo animo pati modo aliquid tam mellitae suavitatis ad eorum aures per-*
> *veniret, tanta dulcedine captos afficit ille animos.*

---

62   George Francis Hill, *A Corpus of Italian Medals of the Renaissance before Cellini,* vol. 1
(London, 1930), plate 79, n. 416.

63   Vatican City, Biblioteca Apostolica Vaticana, MS ottoboniano latino 1153, fol. 128r.

he exulted to no small degree, he cavorted, he could not contain his
joy, he tried to outdo himself when he saw that no one was looking at
Christ, but everyone had turned toward him, and fixed in his gaze,
they marveled at such unheard-of musical allurement that stole each
one's heart away. They were all trampling one another; he worked
upon their captive hearts with such a pleasant charm that they uncom-
plainingly allowed themselves to be knocked down, so long as some of
that honey-sweetness reached their ears.

Pietrobono's enthusiasm grows even greater as the public marvels whether
his hand is guided by a god, wonders what contest there would be between
him and Arion, Timotheum, or Orpheus, and proclaims that even the sun
stops to listen to him. Finally, the ambitious performer and his instrument
succumb to the stress:

> *Cum autem nonnullos audiret ita dicentes: inesse profecto aliquem deum illi*
> *dextrae qui tam celerem motum incitaret, alios hoc modo loquentes: quem Ari-*
> *ona? quem Timotheum? quem Orpheum non contemnimus? alios his verbis*
> *utentes: solem ipsum sui cursus oblitum se inter nubila occultasse ut periboni-*
> *ana harmonia pasceretur, tum vero nova melodiarum genera excogitabatur,*
> *tunc sudor ab eius ore affatim manabat, nervi sufficere non poterant, obrumpe-*
> *bantur chordae prae nimia laudis cupiditate.*

> Then he heard some people saying such things as "Surely there is
> some god in his hand who stirs up such swift motion," and others
> speaking thus: "Do we not scorn any Arion? or Timotheum? or
> Orpheus?" and others using these words: "The sun itself has forgotten
> its course and hidden itself among clouds so that it might feast on
> Pietrobono's harmony." Then indeed he thought up new kinds of
> melodies, then sweat poured freely from his face; his strings could not
> take it, and broke from his excessive desire for praise.

These details provide a colorful backdrop for the eulogy that Aurelio
Brandolini composed for Pietrobono in 1473, when the latter visited
Naples as part of the Este delegation from Ferrara. The original (formerly
in the royal library at Naples) is lost, but the text is available in a copy that
may be identified as (or else may be derived from) the "Musica Lippi" that
was sent from Naples to Lorenzo de' Medici probably around 1480.[64] It
contains the following:

---

64   Lucca, Biblioteca Capitolare, MS 525, fols. 175v–184r; cf. Tammaro de Marinis, *La
biblioteca napoletana dei re d'Aragona* (Milan, 1947–51), vol. 1, pp. 75–77.

1. *Lippi Brandoli[ni] praefatio in Libellum de laudibus musicae et Petriboni-ferrariensis ad summam maiestatem regis Ferdinandi* (see appendix, I)
2. *Ad Petrumbonum* (see appendix, II)
3. *Lippi Brandolini ad serenissimum regem Ferdinandum de laudibus musicae et Petriboni libellus incipit* (see appendix, III)
4. *Eiusdem de laudibus Petriboni* (see appendix, IV)
5. *Eiusdem ad Franciscum Petriboni comitem*
6. *Eiusdem ad Ferdinandum regem* (see appendix, V)
7. *Eiusdem ad Herculem Ferrariae ducem*
8. *Eiusdem ad libellum ut Ferdinandum adeat* (see appendix, VI)
9. *Ioannis Francisci Arcophili posaurensis in laudem Petriboni epigramma*

1. The preface by Lippo Brandolini to his small volume in praise of music and of Pietrobono of Ferrara, addressed to His Most High Majesty King Ferdinand
2. To Pietrobono
3. Here begins the small volume by Lippo Brandolini addressed to the Most Serene King Ferdinand, in praise of music and Pietrobono
4. By the same author, in praise of Pietrobono
5. By the same author, to Francesco, the companion of Pietrobono
6. By the same author, to King Ferdinand
7. By the same author, to Duke Ercole of Ferrara
8. By the same author, to his little book, exhorting it to go to Ferdinand
9. Epigram of Giovanni Francesco Arcofilo of Pisa in praise of Pietrobono

The central sections (nos. 4, 5, and 6) could have come from a performance in praise of Pietrobono and King Ferdinand given by Brandolini at court in the spring of 1473—a concert by a vocal improvisor, whose theme was a concert by an instrumental improvisor. If so, the *Libellus* (no. 3) would be a written elaboration and expansion of Brandolini's original eulogy of Pietrobono (no. 4). With the dedicatory material added in the beginning (nos. 1 and 2) and at the end (nos. 7, 8, and 9), the result is a pamphlet that may even have been intended for publication.

The most important text, the *Libellus de laudibus musicae et Petriboni* (appendix, III) opens with an invocation to Apollo and the Muses, that they might assist the poet in his undertaking (lines 1–24). The beginning of the poem proper offers an unusual glimpse of how a fifteenth-century man of letters viewed the musical situation of his day. He imagines in fact that Jove is greatly pleased when pondering the general state of culture in

Italy (lines 27–30): that which a coarse age [read today: the Middle Ages!] had ignored has been largely recuperated by modern men [read today: the Humanists!] (lines 31–32). Only music in Italy seems dead [read today: the "segreto del Quattrocento"][65] (lines 33–36). Thus Jove decides to remedy this unhappy situation by generating a musician who will revive the art, indeed surpassing the musicians of antiquity (lines 37–40). This new creature is endowed with the best of all physical and moral gifts and furnished with the instruments of his craft, the *plectrum* and *citharam* (lines 41–50) [not pen and paper: the savior of Italian music therefore belongs to "unwritten tradition"!]. His appearance and virtues are fashioned in likeness of Phoebus, so that he is identifiable with Phoebus in every way. The gods even call him by the same name, which the common people then corrupt to "Petrus," adding to it "Bonus" (lines 51–70).

The core of the poem is the celebratory description of a "concert" given by Pietrobono. It is punctuated by a series of imperatives that introduce the various phases of the narration, serving to periodically revive the attention of the reader (or the listener, if this text was also originally improvised): "Pende animo" (Pay close attention: line 79), "Subiice nunc animo" (Attend closely now: line 87), "Aspice" (Look: line 115), and "Adde" (Add to this: line 169). The description focuses first on the swiftness of Pietrobono's left hand as it moves over the strings (lines 79–86), then on the movement of his right hand as it employs the plectrum (lines 87–90), and finally on the alternation and perfect coordination of both hands working together (lines 91–100). With this Brandolini turns to the repertory Pietrobono performed in his concert, pieces of English, French, Spanish, and Italian origin (lines 101–10). Singers and instrumentalists came in fact from many different places to work in the courts of Italy, especially those of Ferrara and Naples, so that Pietrobono could easily have been familiar with music from all over Europe. Next is a description of Pietrobono's interpretative methods, with particular emphasis on his use of rhythmic modifications, added embellishments, and varied motivic repetition (lines 115–32). Here Brandolini tries to imitate such virtuosity

---

65   See Fausto Torrefranca, *Il segreto del Quattrocento. Musiche ariose e poesia popolaresca* (Milan, 1939).

with the tools of his own medium. Thus the same construction is repeated with variation at the beginning of three consecutive distichs:

> *Contrahit attenuatque* . . . (line 117)
> *Decurrit peragitque* . . . (line 119)
> *Itque reditque* . . . (line 121)

The last of these phrases is repeated verbatim at the end of line 122. There are also repetitions of verbal sonorities: between the beginnings of lines 123 ("densentur numeri") and 124 ("densentur simili"); and between the middle of line 125 ("magis atque magis") and the beginning and end of line 126 ("quo magis . . . illa magis"). The distinct general impression is, in any case, that Pietrobono would produce a highly embellished *cantus* with his instrument. The musical support, which also served to highlight Pietrobono's improvisational ability, was an unvaried *tenor* provided by his faithful accompanist (lines 133–40), "fidus in arte comes, fidus amore magis" (faithful companion in art, even more faithful in love; the nature of this love is more fully addressed in composition no. 5, which is dedicated to Pietrobono's accompanist and companion, Francesco Malacise). After several other observations concerning the types of variation and the imitative technique used by Pietrobono (lines 141–68), the description closes by returning to the physical person and his ability to use gestures effectively in his performance (lines 169–74). This practice of accompanying certain moments of the musical performance with appropriate gestures was a traditional precept that had been carried over to music from the *pronuntiatio* of rhetoric.[66]

At this point Brandolini finds himself forced to admit that verbal language is unable to render a complete account of this extraordinary musical event (lines 175–80). Beyond the rhetorical justification, there was in fact a genuine problem that had several different aspects. First of all, the language: as has been observed regarding the verbal rendering of pictorial experiences,[67] the vocabulary and syntax of Latin then in use strongly conditioned the possibilities and methods of description; sufficient proof of

66   Gallo, "Pronuntiatio."
67   Michael Baxandall, *Giotto and the Orators: Humanist Observers of Painting in Italy and the Discovery of Pictorial Composition 1350–1450* (Oxford, 1971), pp. 8–50.

this can be found by comparing eulogies of Pietrobono in Latin with those written in Italian.[68] Then there was the relationship between poetic—or in any case literary—language and technical language; nearly everything Brandolini actually says about music in two hundred lines of verse can be had in these few lines written by the contemporary "Neapolitan" theoretician and composer, Johannes Tinctoris:

> *nonnulli associati supremam partem cuiusvis compositi cantus cum admiran-*
> *dis modulorum superinventionibus adeo eleganter ea personant, ut profecto*
> *nihil prestantius . . . inter quos Petrus Bonus Herculis Ferrarie ducis incliti*
> *lyricen (mea quidem sententia) ceteris est preferendus.*[69]

> some associates play the high part of any composed piece whatsoever with amazing invention of modulations, so elegantly that surely nothing is more excellent . . . among whom Pietrobono, the *lyra* player of the renowned Duke Ercole of Ferrara, is (in my decided opinion) to be preferred to all others.

And finally, a centuries-old tradition was broken: in this epoch there was perhaps a profound transformation in the paradigms of listening to music, certainly in the paradigms adopted for the verbal description of that listening. In the fourteenth century, listening to music still inevitably suggested images of performing angels, of inner rapture.[70] But the orators of the fifteenth century had a completely different field of reference: in listening to music they thought only of Orpheus, Amphion, and Apollo. The same Tinctoris, a musician and music theoretician who was very much a part of the culture of his time, could not help but place Pietrobono in a line of descent leading directly back to those names of antiquity.[71]

In closing his poem, Brandolini turns personally to Pietrobono and invites him to choose King Ferdinand over all other potentates who would have him in their service (lines 191–200). There are further remarks along the same lines in the introductory prose (no. 1) and the verses

---

68   Nino Pirrotta, "Musica e orientamenti culturali nell'Italia del Quattrocento," in *Musica tra Medioevo e Rinascimento* (Turin, 1984), pp. 213–49.

69   Karl Weinmann, *Johannes Tinctoris (1445–1511) und sein unbekannter Traktat "De inventione et usu musicae"* (Regensburg, 1917), p. 45.

70   F. Alberto Gallo, "Dal Duecento al Quattrocento," in *Letteratura italiana*, ed. Alberto Asor Rosa, vol. 6 (Turin, 1986), pp. 259–63.

71   Weinmann, *Johannes Tinctoris,* pp. 43–45.

addressed to Ferdinand (no. 6), where Brandolini theorizes the perfect equivalency between the king and his preferred court musician, basing it on the usual comparison with the ancients. For Ferdinand emulates with his virtues

> *omnes non modo romanos, verum etiam graecos et totius orbis reges ac principes.*

> all the kings and princes, not only of Rome, but also of Greece and of the entire world.

Even if one considers only those virtues that are practiced in times of peace—prudence, magnanimity, moderation, and, above all, justice—he is

> *sine ulla dubitatione veteribus omnibus aut praestantior . . . aut certe non inferior.*

> without any doubt, either superior to all the ancients . . . or at least certainly not inferior to them.

And with regard to his study of the liberal arts,

> *quas tu quidem quantum amaveris quantumque in illis profeceris (ut de reliquis taceamus) musica maximo documento est, quum nec veterum nec recentiorum principum quisquis eius rei fuerit studiosior.*

> music (not to mention the others) provides the best example of how much you love them and how proficient you have become in them, since not any of the ancient or modern princes has been more studious of this art.

Pietrobono for his part

> *. . . Dircaeum et Ariona vincit*
> *Orpheaque et Phoebo te, Line clare, tuo.*

> . . . vanquishes the Dircaean [Amphion], and Arion,
> And Orpheus, and you, fair Linus, are surpassed by your Phoebus.

In the opinion of everyone, but above all of the king, he is a "musicus . . . praestantissimus" (most excellent musician). The occasion of Leonora's marriage therefore brought the finest musician to the court of the greatest ruler:

> *Haud alia tu dignus eras, rex maxime, musa:*
> *hic quo non alio te nisi dignus erat.*

> It would hardly have been worthy of you, O greatest king, to have any other muse:
> this one was worthy of no one other than you.

The position of excellence each holds in his respective field makes for a sort of ideal equality between lord and artist:

> *Praestantes optas, nam praestantissimus ipse es:*
> *coniunctos paribus sic decet esse pares.*

> You choose those who are outstanding because you yourself are the
>   most outstanding;
> it is fitting that equals be thus joined to equals.

This is no small recognition of the level of human and social dignity that a musician could reach, albeit exceptionally; indeed, Tinctoris was able to write, at the time, that music "peritos in ea glorificat"[72] (gives glory to those who are skilled in it). It is worth noting further that Iuniano Maio, professor of rhetoric at the University of Naples, would later dedicate to Ferdinand a treatise entitled *De maiestate* in which "majesty" is considered an attribute of music as well as royalty:

> *Non con manco dignitate se sole attribuire questa alma Maiestate anco a le bone*
> *e sublime scienze, a la eloquenza, a la musica, a la aritmetica et a le altre.*[73]

> It is not a lack of respect if I am wont to attribute this spirit of Majesty
> also to the good and sublime sciences, to eloquence, to music, to
> arithmetic, and to others.

There is some possibility that the entire pamphlet was conceived as a gift from Aurelio Brandolini (and obviously the king) to Pietrobono, as the dedication to Pietrobono (no. 2) suggests. After all, Ercole d'Este could consider himself more than satisfied with the acquisition of Leonora of Aragon and leave Pietrobono to Ferdinand, as the last line of the verses addressed to Ercole (no. 7) states:

> *at data pro Petro sit Leonora tibi.*

> but let Leonora be given to you in place of Pietro.

Ferdinand's attempt to obtain the famous instrumentalist from Ferrara was not successful on this occasion, but he apparently did not stop there: again in 1476 Diomede Carafa, secretary to the king, wrote to Ercole that

---

72   F. Alberto Gallo, *La polifonia del Medioevo* (Turin, 1991), p. 91; English edition, *Music of the Middle Ages II* (Cambridge, 1985), p. 81.
73   Iuniano Maio, *De maiestate,* ed. Franco Gaeta (Bologna, 1956), p. 16.

"la Maestà de lo Signore Re averia multo piacere" (His Majesty the King would be greatly pleased) if Pietrobono were to return to Naples.[74]

The other, shorter composition in praise of Pietrobono (no. 4) contains an interesting development of the topos "Orpheum superans" (triumphant over Orpheus). It is true that Orpheus and Amphion could use their music to force mountains and beasts, stones and walls to do their will (lines 1–4, 15–16), but these marvelous effects only proved that the simple and inexperienced are easily attracted by any ability, even a mediocre one (lines 17–20). Pietrobono's merit is infinitely greater, since he weaves his spell over noble and cultured people (lines 23–26), "proceres regesque peritos" (princes and kings who are experts). Therefore his art is cultured in like measure as his admiring public: "qui flectit doctos, hic mihi doctus erit" (he who sways the learned, this is the one who in my eyes is learned); the concert at the castle is not only a diversion but also a cultural experience. In effect, the extraordinary virtuosity with which Pietrobono elaborated a *cantus* from musical motives that his accompanist provided in the *tenor* (an immediately perceptible form of polyphony) may have brought his listeners to an increased awareness of musical technique, and alerted them to the fact that only with adequate musical preparation could they fully enjoy the performance. No doubt Battista Guarini had Pietrobono in mind when he wrote this observation in *De ordine docendi ac studendi:*

> *pulsante optimo citharoedo magis delectatur qui eius artis cognitionem aliquam attingit quam qui ignorat.*[75]

> one who has attained some knowledge of his art enjoys the playing of an excellent citharist more than one who is ignorant.

And it is interesting that Aurelio Brandolini himself, in an analogous work entitled *De ratione scribendi,* should find a way to generalize this same need for proper background:

> *in musica minima quaeque deprehandere nisi peritissimus artis non potest.*[76]

> in music, no one who is not very skilled in the art is able to grasp even the least things.

---

74   Lewis Lockwood, "Pietrobono and the Instrumental Tradition at Ferrara in the Fifteenth Century," *Rivista italiana di musicologia* 10 (1975): 127–28.

75   Battista Guarini, *De ordine docendi ac studendi* (Ferrara, 1474).

76   Aurelio Brandolini, *De ratione scribendi libri tres* (Rome, 1735), p. 298.

III

In Ferrara, Guarino Veronese delivered two important academic orations: one for the reopening of the *studium generale,* under the patronage of Leonello d'Este, in 1442;[77] and the other five years later, inaugurating courses for 1447.[78] These orations eulogize the various disciplines taught at the university; the youthful scholars are exhorted to study so that they might avail themselves of the utility to be gained from the mastery of these disciplines; and in conclusion Guarino extols Leonello, who provides the moral and material support for the institution. There is no mention of music, since it was not taught at the university. Nonetheless, it rightfully belonged to the traditional scholastic system of the seven liberal arts, and Guarino's students, who were personally interested in the practice of music, did find a way to include musical references in their own orations.

Thus in 1453 Battista Guarini would devote considerable space to the praise of music in a speech he gave before Borso d'Este, with citations and examples taken from Greek and Latin literature:[79] first he recalled the inventors of the theory and practice of music, then its wondrous effects, with prominence given to Timotheus and a citation from Aristotle's *Politics.* At this point the eighteen-year-old Battista posed a question to his public, which consisted largely of students his same age:

> *sed quid huius rei ab antiquis argumenta requirimus? credo enim omnes, qui in hoc celebratissimo hominum conventu adsunt, nonnumquam in choreis nostris adnotasse quodam cantus genere celeriores, quodam vero tardiores incedere saltantes.*

> but why are we looking for clarification in this matter from the ancients? for I believe that all those present in this most celebrated gathering have observed at some time or other in our dances rather fast songs of a certain kind, to which, however, the dancers step rather slowly.

To appreciate the characteristics of music, there was truly no need for his audience to imagine that of antiquity; it was sufficient to refer to an everyday experience such as dance at court. As circumstance would have it, during those

77   Remigio Sabbadini, "Una prolusione di Guarino Veronese sulle arti liberali," *La biblioteca delle scuole italiane* 7 (1897): 33–35.

78   Karl Müllner, "Acht Inauguralreden des Veronesers Guarino und seines Sohnes Battista," *Wiener Studien* 18 (1896): 298–302.

79   Ibid., 19 (1897): 131–32.

same years Domenico da Piacenza, the most famous fifteenth-century composer of, and author on, balls and dances, was working at the Este court.[80]

Still more extended and impassioned is the eulogy of music (not to
mention painting) that Ludovico Carboni inserted in his oration for the
nomination of a new rector of students (ca. 1458–60):

> quae quidem duae res, musica scilicet et perspectiva, nullo modo inter mechani-
> cas artes connumerandae sunt, cum a verissimarum disciplinarum fundamen-
> tis oriantur, quae apud maiores nostros et latinos et graecos summo in precio et
> honore fuerunt, quibus et clarissimi principes incredibiliter sunt delectati.[81]

> these two things indeed—music, that is, and perspective—are in no
> way to be numbered among the mechanical arts, since they arise from
> the foundations of those most true disciplines that were most highly
> valued and honored among our ancestors both Latin and Greek, and
> in which the most illustrious princes took incredible delight.

Precisely because the arts of music and painting tended particularly to enjoy
princely favor, at this point the author turned directly to Borso, present at
the ceremony, to lament the fact that there was no longer a *cappella musicale*,[82] which had been so diligently maintained by his predecessor Leonello:

> quo magis de te certe miratus sum, inclyte dux, qui cum omni genere laudis
> antecessores vuos superare contendas, hoc solum negligere videaris, quia musi-
> cos, id est cantores, illos apud te non retinueris, qui totiens divinis modulan-
> tionibus suis et angelicis cantibus pulcherrimum hoc templum impleverunt. Si
> quid esse in me facundiae sentirem, totam libenter in eo consumerem, ut tibi
> persuaderem atque in mentem ponerem, revocandos esse omnino musicos ad
> maximam populi tui delectationem.

> all the more am I quite amazed at you, O renowned duke, that while
> you strive to surpass your predecessors in every kind of praiseworthy
> endeavor, you seem to neglect this one alone, because you do not
> maintain at your court those musicians—that is, singers—who daily
> filled this most beautiful temple with their divine melodies and angelic
> singing. If I thought I had any eloquence at all, I would gladly use it all
> to persuade you and settle it firmly in your mind that, above all, these
> musicians should be recalled, to the great delight of your people.

---

80   Lewis Lockwood, *Music in Renaissance Ferrara 1400–1505* (Oxford, 1984), pp.
70–72, 178.
81   Vatican City, Biblioteca Apostolica Vaticana, MS Ottoboniano latino 1153, fol. 189r.
82   Lockwood, *Music in Renaissance Ferrara*, p. 95.

In concluding this section of his speech, Carboni expressed the hope that he might one day possess the material means to demonstrate to everyone his passion for music and painting, second only to his passion for literature:

> *nec ob aliam causam cupio ego dari mihi aliquando magnam fortunam, nisi ut omnibus hominibus apertissime possim ostendere qualis sit animus meus erga musicos et pictores, post litteras tamen, quae meae deliciae sunt.*

> for no other reason do I wish that someday a great fortune might be given to me, but that I might be able to show to all, very clearly, what is my attitude toward musicians and painters—after literature, however, which is my delight.

Besides teaching at the university, Carboni also engaged in diplomatic activities on behalf of Borso, who was lavish in his compensation for this service. Carboni consequently took every possible opportunity to thank his patron, as when he wrote the *Dialogus de septem litteris huius nominis "Borsius,"*[83] in which he used each of the letters of the duke's name as the first letter of one of his virtues:

Bonitas	goodness
Orationis venustas	comeliness of speech
Religio	religion
Sobrietas	temperance
Iustitia	justice
Venustas corporis	comeliness of body
Sagacitas	wisdom

The letters are seven, an important number in the arrangement of the macrocosmos and the microcosmos. Even the human pulse was thought to possess a septenary musical rhythm:

> *Et venas sive pectoris arterias medicomusici dicunt numero moveri septenario, quod ipsi appellant* διὰ τοῦ τεσσάρου συνφωνίαν.

> And the medico-musicians say that the veins, or the arteries of the chest, move to a count of seven, in their terminology, "on account of the consonance of the fourth."

---

83   *Ludovici Carboni Dialogus de septem litteris huius nominis Borsius,* Vatican City, Biblioteca Apostolica Vaticana, MS vaticano latino 8618, fol. 23v; cf. Alfonso Lazzari, "Un dialogo di Ludovico Carbone in lode del duca Borso," *Atti e memorie della Deputazione ferrarese di storia patria* 24 (1919): 3–44.

Actually the "consonance of the fourth" is based on the harmonic ratio of 4 to 3, and not the sum of these two numbers as the author suggests. In 1460 Carboni gave an inaugural speech in which he was able to reaffirm his passion for music—"delector ego . . . vehementer in hac" (I enjoy . . . it immensely)[84]—and to close with a commendation of Borso d'Este (present on this occasion as well) for carrying on Leonello's patronage of the university.

Academic inaugurations were still more frequent at Ferrara during the reign of Ercole d'Este. In 1476 the task of giving the inaugural oration for the academic year was entrusted to the eighteen-year-old Rudolph Agricola, who was not only a student of the *Artes* but also organist of the court *cappella*.[85] The words Agricola dedicated to music eulogize Ercole's interest in the art—"De musica quid attinet dicere post illustrissimi principis nostri iudicium?" (What is there to say of any importance about music, after the judgment of our most illustrious prince?)—while clearly alluding to the condition of the professional musician—"ne ipse placere mihi studiisque meis mollius videar esse blanditus" (lest I seem to be pleased with myself and gently flattering toward my studies).[86]

Ludovico Carboni's relationship with Ercole was not as felicitous as the one he had enjoyed with Borso. Certainly the name "Hercules" was far less conducive to celebratory literary exercises—if anything, it was better suited for musical ones, as Josquin Desprez would demonstrate with his Mass on the name "Hercules dux Ferrarie."[87] Carboni's academic inaugural oration in 1478 (for which Ercole was present), though extended, follows formulae by then become common and limits the praise of music, as well as the other disciplines, to a single adjective:

> *pura grammatica, acuta dialettica, ornata rhetorica, distinta arithmetica, suavis musica, certa geometria, sublimis astronomia, subtilis philosophia, salutaris medicina, severe leges, mirabilis theologia.*[88]

---

84   Bologna, Biblioteca Universitaria, MS 2948, t. 34, p. 371.

85   Lockwood, *Music in Renaissance Ferrara*, pp. 151–52.

86   Hans Rupprich, *Humanismus und Renaissance in den deutschen Städten und an den Universitäten* (Leipzig, 1935), p. 177.

87   Lockwood, *Music in Renaissance Ferrara*, pp. 241–49.

88   Bologna, Biblioteca Universitaria, MS 2948, t. 34, fol. 289.

plain grammar, keen dialectics, ornate rhetoric, distinct arithmetic, sweet music, certain geometry, lofty astronomy, subtle philosophy, health-giving medicine, stern law, awesome theology.

Guarino's teaching may have particularly encouraged the inclusion of musical references in the academic orations at Ferrara, but it is not impossible to find analogous cases in Naples. Here it was that the *studium generale* was reopened by Alfonso of Aragon, and here Gregorio da Città di Castello, who was at Alfonso's court between 1447 and 1450,[89] probably gave the inaugural oration. In the prologue he addresses the problem of how this type of speech should be organized so that it might correspond to the particular exigencies of the context and the audience, and this subject immediately offers him the means of introducing a rhetorical comparison with music. The musician

> *in arte sua pro hominum natura atque animorum diversitate nunc acrem nunc levem nunc gravem cantum modulatur.*[90]

> in his art, because of the nature of people and the diversity of their spirits, plays sometimes a poignant, sometimes a light, sometimes a serious song.

Therefore, so that this oration might avoid the pattern usually followed for a generic eulogy of the various disciplines, Gregorio proposes to address a specific theme: "de affinitate et cognatione scientiarum" (concerning the interconnection and relationship of the sciences). In so doing he reveals a strong affinity between oratory and poetry, but above all between poetry and music:

> *at nihil omnino differt ab oratore poeta, nisi quod liberius ei licet evagari et paulo numeris est astrictior magisque ad concentum quendam et musicam accedit; unde poetica musica dicitur et Musis est consacrata: idcirco poetam non solum musicae rationem, sed etiam usum habere oportet; quo modo enim tam multa exercebit, quae pertinent ad poetam?*[91]

> but the poet differs not at all from the orator except that he is allowed to range more freely, is somewhat more concise with regard to meter,

---

89   Louis Delaruelle, "Une vie d'humaniste au XVe Siècle," *Mélanges d'archeologie et d'histoire* 19 (1899): 9–33.

90   Karl Müllner, *Reden und Briefe italienischer Humanisten* (Vienna, 1899), p. 182.

91   Ibid., p. 187.

and more closely approaches a kind of consonance, and music; hence poetry is called music, and is consecrated to the Muses. For this reason the poet should not only have a command of the theory of music but should also be skilled in practice, for how else will he exercise many of the skills that pertain to poetry?

Contemporary improvisors and singers of Latin verses no doubt offered the ideal realization of this affinity. Equally strong, even if more traditional and widely taken for granted, is the connection between mathematics and music:

> *nam quid aliud est musica quam numerus quidam? quapropter concentus et musicae ratio numerus appellatur, quod ea numero mensuretur et numero constet.*[92]

for what is music but a certain kind of measure? Therefore the underlying structure of harmony and music is called number, for it is measured by number and consists of number.

When Gregorio then turns specifically to the discipline of music, he immediately expresses his sadness over its current state of abandonment:

> *musicam a nostris neglectam atque ignoratam doleo, sive id propter eius difficultatem magnitudinemque evenerit, sive propter hominum cupiditatem atque desidiam.*[93]

I grieve that music is neglected and unknown among our people, whether this has come about because of the difficulty and magnitude of the subject or because of people's greed and laziness.

The ancients, in contrast, had held music in high regard for its marvelous effects on humans, animals, and even inanimate objects. He concludes, returning to the theme of the oration proper, that music has affinities with philosophy, poetry, arithmetic, and, in a singular fashion, with rhetoric:

> *addamus etiam hoc, quod fortasse mirum videatur, colores in musica inveniri rhetoricis coloribus similes, ut repetitionem, frequentationem et alios complures.*[94]

let me also add this, which may perhaps seem surprising: in music we find stylistic devices similar to those in rhetoric, such as repetition, cumulative effects, and many others.

92 Ibid., p. 188.
93 Ibid., p. 189.
94 Ibid., p. 190.

It must be remembered that there was a treatise on poetics and rhetoric dating from this same period by Giacomo Borbo, *maestro di canto* for the *cappella* of Alfonso of Aragon.[95]

Antonio Campano, who had studied at the University of Naples during the reign of Alfonso and then entered the service of the Baglioni family, lords of Perugia, wrote an inaugural oration for the year 1455 at the University of Perugia that contains an extended eulogy of music. After the usual citations of relevant ancient writings, he presents the current definition of music as

> *rem praterea ad animi atque aurium delectationem mirifice accomodatam.*[96]
>
> a thing above all admirably suited to delight the soul and the ear.

Another oration, *De laudibus litterarum* by Giovanni Brancati,[97] was delivered in Naples in 1468 before King Ferdinand of Aragon, who had always devoted considerable attention to the development of the Neapolitan *studium generale*. Brancati, Ferdinand's court librarian, explicates the academic court character and function of his speech, professing to pursue the twofold purpose of praising both the various disciplines and the king's virtues ("in laudandis vel disciplinis vel regis virtutibus"). However, several disciplines, among them music, are barely mentioned: "disciplinas quas Graeci mathematicas vocant: arithmeticam, geometriam, musicam, astrologiam" (disciplines that the Greeks call mathematical: arithmetic, geometry, music, astrology).

Andrea Brenta, in service to Cardinal Oliviero Carafa of Naples (to whom Aurelio Brandolini would dedicate an oration in honor of St. Thomas), instead inserted an enthusiastic eulogy of music in an inaugural oration dating from 1474 and delivered in Rome. Among the usual citations taken from the ancient authors (here again a quote from Aristotle's *Politics* assumes particular significance) is this marked invitation to music as a practical part of contemporary life:

---

95   F. Alberto Gallo, "Musica, poetica e retorica nel Quattrocento: L'*Illuminator* di Giacomo Borbo," *Rivista italiana di musicologia* 10 (1975): 72–85.

96   *Antonii Campani Opera* (Rome, 1495).

97   De Marinis, *La biblioteca napoletana*, vol. 1, pp. 247–51.

nos utique illam amplecti oportet sine qua vita nostra multa delectabili, hon-
esta et prope necessaria voluptate careret.[98]

it especially behooves us to embrace that without which our life would
be lacking in much delightful, wholesome, and indeed, all but necessary, pleasure.

These are the precedents for the oration that Aurelio Brandolini
delivered at Capua before Ferdinand of Aragon, inaugurating the academic year 1478–79. The surviving manuscript of the speech preserves it in a
bilingual format: Latin (the language in which it was probably given) and
Italian (in all likelihood a translation done by the author himself).[99]

Brandolini begins by recalling that it is customary to initiate the academic
year by urging scholars to rally themselves round the various areas of study:

Num cum, et tempus ipsum eiusmodi sit, quo singulis annis ad studia
bonarum artium liberalesque disciplinas summo studio capessandas omnes
hortari atque incitari et soleant et debeant, et ego sim in hac civitate ad traden-
das omnibus litteras a tua maiestate constitutus, putavi ad officium meae pro-
fessionis pertinere, ut aliquid hoc tempore dicerem.

Venendo el tempo che ogni anno si suole et debbe confortare et incitare
ciaschuno ad prendere con grande studio et diligentia li studij de le buone arte
e liberale discipline, ed essendo io dall'altro canto per ordine di tua maiestà ad
insignar littere a tutti in questa città consituito, mi parve che allo offitio della
professione et exercitio mio s'appartenesse dire al presente alcuna cosa.[100]

The moment having come when each year it is usual and obligatory to
support and encourage each person to take up with great application
and diligence the study of the fine arts and liberal disciplines, and
since I have been charged by Your Majesty to teach literature to all in
this city, it seemed to me pertinent to the office of my profession and
practice to say something at this time.

He also recalls that this type of oration usually consists of either presenting and praising a chosen discipline, or rapidly mentioning each and
every one of them:

98   Müllner, *Reden und Briefe*, p. 78.

99   Paris, Bibliothèque Nationale, MS latin 7860. The Latin and Italian are usually quite
close, and only one English translation is given. When, occasionally, there is a divergence,
the translation tends to follow the Italian. Cf. M. G. Di Pierro, "Una inedita controversia di
Lippo Brandolini sul primato fra le lettere e le armi alla corte di Ferrante d'Aragona," *Annali*
della Facoltà di Lettere e Filosofia, Università degli Studi di Bari 24 (1981): 401–19.

100   Paris, Bibliothèque Nationale, MS latin 7860, fols. 6r, 42v.

nonnulli de singulis disciplinis dicere parum putantes, dicere de universis
conantur.

alcuni parendo loro poco de una scientia ragionare si sforzano fare di tutte
menzione.[101]

some, thinking it too little to speak of one science, endeavor to mention them all.

In light of current social reality, however, Brandolini intends here to take a
new and different path: to speak of the relationship between literary studies and military life, thereby taking on a theme that was hotly debated
throughout the fifteenth century.[102] Actually, the author had already
touched on this subject in the brief poem praising music and Pietrobono
discussed above (appendix, V). There the famous instrumentalist is cred-
ited with being able to cause cultural values to prevail over the use of arms:

Hic trahit a bellis summos ad carmina reges,
doctior hic armis, nam toga docta magis.

He draws the great kings from warfare to songs;
he is more learned than arms, for the toga is the more learned.

Paraphrasing here Cicero's famous "cedant arma togae"[103] (may arms give
way to the toga), Brandolini seems at this time to have embraced the idea
that literature is superior to arms. But in the oration at Capua he seems
instead to favor a perspective of substantial equilibrium between them.

Brandolini first illustrates the great esteem the ancients had for the
liberal disciplines, an esteem that was already evident in their debate over
the invention of each individual discipline. For music in particular:

De musicae etiam inventione veteres dubitavere. Nam alij ab Amphione, alij
Mercurio, nonnulli ab Apolline inventam existimaverunt. Proptereaquod
Apollinem cum cythara veteres poetae finxerunt.

Dubitorno ancora li antichi della inventione de la musica, attento che molti
estimarono essere stata da Amphione trovata. Alcuni altri Mercurio, altri

---

101   Ibid., fols. 6v, 43r.
102   *Sapere e/è potere: Discipline, dispute e professioni nell'università medievale e moderna: Il caso*
bolognese a confronto, vol. 1 ed. Luisa Avellini, vol. 2 ed. Andrea Cristiani, vol. 3 ed. Angela de
Benedictis (Bologna, 1990).
103   *De officiis,* 1.77.

Apolline ne fecero inventore, et però finxero li antichi poeti Apolline cola cithara.[104]

The ancients were also uncertain about the invention of music, since many thought it to have been discovered by Amphion. Several others made Mercury the inventor, others Apollo; therefore the ancient poets portrayed Apollo with the cithara.

He then goes on to examine the importance that martial art has in the defense of justice, as a safeguard for respect of the law and therefore indispensable to social order and evolution. And he recalls the esteem it too enjoyed in ancient times, mentioning the great military leaders of antiquity. But the central theme of the oration is a demonstration that these two activities, though apparently unrelated, can and must work together. Literary culture is not just a matter of personal, private enrichment, but also a powerful influence upon the external world, upon the whole of society. Indeed, what do the great musical myths of antiquity signify, if not the beneficial influence of culture on the civil and moral development of humanity?

Atque hinc poetae veteres cecinerunt Orpheum feras et saxa cantus dulcedine attraxisse. Hinc Amphion cythara thebanos muros aedificasse. . . . Nam quid, obsecro, aliud est feras et saxa dulcedine carminis demulceri nisi rusticos atque agrestes homines Orphei sapientissimi viri doctrina et eloquentia informari? Quid aliud est Amphionem cithara thebanos muros aedificare nisi doctum atque eloquentem virum rusticis atque incultis hominibus sua sapientia persuadere ut in coetu ac societate vivant, moenia aedificent, civitatemque conficiant?

Et per questo dissero li antichi poeti che Orpheo con la dulceza del suo canto haveva tirato ad andare le fere et saxi. Per questo disero che Amphion con la cythera haveva le mura di Tebe edificate. . . . Imperoché che vuole dire altro le fere et li saxi essere dalla dulceza del canto mollificati, se non che li huomini rustici et inculti sono dirozzati et ammaestrati dalla doctrina et eloquentia d'Orpheo sapientissimo huomo? Che vuole dir altro Amphione edificare cola cythera li mura thebani, se non che un docto et eloquente uomo con la sua sapientia dà ad intendere ad huomini rustici e grossi che vivano insieme et in congregatione, che edificheno muri et facciano una città?[105]

And so the ancient poets said that Orpheus, with the sweetness of his song, was able to move wild beasts and stones. So too they said that Amphion with the cithara built the walls of Thebes. . . . For what else

104   Paris, Bibliothèque Nationale, MS latin 7860, fols. 19r, 57r.
105   Ibid., fols. 23v, 62v.

could wild beasts and stones being softened by the sweetness of song
mean, if not that rustic and uncultured men are refined and trained
by the teaching and eloquence of Orpheus, a most wise man? What
else could Amphion building the walls of Thebes with the cithara
mean, if not that a learned and eloquent man with his wisdom per-
suades rustic and unrefined men to live together in society, to build
walls and construct a city?

It is interesting to note that Ludovico Carboni had proposed the same
interpretation in one of his own dialogues:

> *Quid enim aliud Orphei lyra et Amphionis cithara prae se ferunt qui arbores qui*
> *saxa qui fluvios ad cantum suum traxisse dicunt? Scilicet haud poterant quae sint*
> *sine permovere sensu finxere docti fabulas poetae quod rudes et imperitos homines*
> *arboribus et saxis comparandos ab agresti et fera illa vita revocarunt atque ad hunc*
> *civilem humanumque cultum deduxerunt, ferocia corda blanda voce mitigantes*
> *persuadentesque satius esset ut omnes in una moenia convenirent.*[106]

For what else do they mean by the lyra of Orpheus and the cithara of
Amphion, who say that Orpheus and Amphion drew trees and stones
and rivers to their song? Surely they could hardly move things that
were without sense; the learned poets devised fables because they
called rude and ignorant people—to be compared to trees and
stones—away from their rough and wild life and led them to this civi-
lized and humane culture, softening fierce hearts by their soothing
voice and persuading them that it was preferable that all come
together within the one wall.

This interpretation served primarily to ennoble and glorify precisely those
two arts, oratory and song, that personages like Brandolini and Carboni
plied on a daily basis. However, its origins can be found in these famous
lines by Horace:

> *Silvestres homines sacer interpresque deorum*
> *caedibus et victu foedo deterruit Orpheus,*
> *dictus ob hoc lenire tigris reabidosque leones;*
> *dictus et Amphion, Thebanae conditor urbis,*
> *saxa movere sono testudinis et prece blanda*
> *ducere quo vellet. Fuit haec sapientia quondam,*[107]

---

106   *Ludovici Carbonis Dialogus de felicitate Ferrariae,* Vatican City, Biblioteca Apostolica Vaticana, MS vaticano latino 8618, fol. 88v.
107   *De arte poetica,* 391–96.

> Orpheus, priest and interpreter of the gods,
> deterred the woods-people from slaughter and their dreadful way of life;
> on account of this he was said to tame tigers and raging lions;
> and Amphion, founder of the city of Thebes,
> was said to move stones by the sound of his instrument and by his
>   soothing entreaty
> to lead them where he would. This was the wisdom of times past

—lines that Tinctoris would faithfully quote when writing about Pietro-bono and other virtuosos of the "*lyra.*"[108]

Having thus demonstrated the social value of culture, Brandolini goes on to assert that a knowledge of the liberal arts can be important for the military commander as well:

> *Quid dicam de bonarum artium studijs ac liberalibus disciplinis? Nonne sunt hae quoque imperatori maxime necessarie?*
>
> *Che dirò delli studij delle bone arte et delle discipline liberale? Non sono loro ancora al capitano grandemente necessarie?*[109]
>
> What am I to say of the fine arts and of the liberal disciplines? Are they not also of great necessity to the commander?

He does not dwell on particular examples, perhaps because the subject had already been specifically addressed by Roberto Valturio in *De re militari*, a treatise that was well known in Neapolitan circles (even the manuscript copy for Matthias Corvinus of Hungary was prepared by a scribe in service at the Aragon court, Joan Marco Cinico).[110] Valturio's work, which was written in 1460 for Sigismondo Pandolfo Malatesta and therefore produced in a courtly environment, illustrates in its first sections how useful it is for a commander to be familiar with literature, the liberal arts, the disciplines of university study. In the chapter devoted to music (which includes the usual series of examples taken from antiquity), Valturio stresses the recreational function of listening to music:

> *Nam si uti tu tecum aliquando soles, sapientissime princeps, post magnas curas, difficiles et illustres occupationes relaxandi ac reparandi animi gratia, vel amicorum vel propter virtutem quis agat, non illiberaliter sed modeste ab his*

---

108   Weinmann, *Johannes Tinctoris*, p. 44.
109   Paris, Bibliothèque Nationale, MS latin 7860, fols. 33v, 75r.
110   De Marinis, *La biblioteca napoletana*, vol. 1, p. 51.

aliquid voluptatis assumet nec absurde hanc musicae artem bellicae fortitudini
coniunxisse te quispiam admiretur.

Si come tu qualche fiata sei usato fare dopoi le grandi toe malenconie et difficile
et illustre di bataglie occupatione per cagione di recreare l'animo tuo over di
amici over per cagione di virtute non paciamente ma modestamente da quelli
suoni qualche piacere prenderà né inconvenevolmente questa arte de' suoni a di
bataglia la forcia te havere coniuntto alcuno si meravelie.[111]

If after your great cares and difficult and illustrious territorial battles,
in order to relax your spirit, or that of your friends, or for reasons of
virtue, you sometimes are accustomed to take some pleasure, not
ignobly but moderately, in those sounds, let no one unreasonably marvel that you have combined this art of sounds with the force of battle.

Behind this one can always discern the image of Homer's (and Vergerio's
and Guarino's) Achilles, who sings after battle; and in the final analysis
Brandolini too proposes the same ideal of a great military leader who is
also a lover of the arts. This model could be found in many commanders
of antiquity, but it persists still in Brandolini's own day. One brilliant
example is that of the duke of Urbino, Federico da Montefeltro, whom
the orator may have come to know in Naples (as we have seen) just a few
years earlier:

Venio ad imperatores nostri temporis. Fredericus Urbinas. Nonne imperator est
nostra aetate praestantissimus? Nonne idem etiam in liberalibus disciplinis
peritissimus? Adeo ut etiam non mediocris philosophus testatur?

Non è Federico duca d'Orbino alla aetà nostra eccellentissimo capitano? Non è
esso ancora nele discipline liberali doctissimo? Per modo che è ancora non
mediocre philosopho reputato.[112]

Now I come to the commanders of our time. Is not Federico, duke of
Urbino, a most excellent commander of our age? Is he not also most
learned in the liberal disciplines? To such an extent that he is also
reputed to be a not mediocre philosopher?

But why look elsewhere, Brandolini concludes, when the most illustrious
example of victorious warrior combined with patron of the arts is embod-
ied in King Ferdinand himself, present at this ceremony?

111   Roberto Valturio, *De re militari* (Verona, 1472); Italian translation by Paolo Ramusio
(Verona, 1483). (English translation from the Italian.)
112   Paris, Bibliothèque Nationale, MS latin 7860, fols. 38v, 81r.

Nonne tu, Ferdinande rex sapientissime, quantus imperator et sis et fueris non huius regni totiusque Italiae modo, sed universae quoque Europae testimonio facile confirmari potest? Quanta autem et juri civili et philosophiae et ceteris liberalium artium studijs ab ineunte aetate operam dederis . . .

Quanto grande et excellente capitano et sia stato et al presente sia tu, Ferdinando re sapientissimo, si può facilmente provare per testimonio non solamente di questo regno et di tutta la Italia, ma ancora di tutta la Europa. Quanta opera tu habia ancora data da la tua tenera et puerile aetate et ale legge civile et alla philosophia et all'altre discipline liberale . . .[113]

How great and excellent a commander you have been and are now, O most wise king Ferdinand, can be easily proven by testimonial coming not only from this kingdom and from all of Italy, but also from all of Europe. How much attention have you also given from a young and tender age to civil laws and to philosophy, and to the other liberal disciplines . . .

This concept and even some of the identical wording can also be found in Brandolini's preface for his Italian translation of Pliny's *Panegyric on Trajan*, dedicated to Ferdinand that same year.[114] But here, in this oration at Capua, the emphasis lies not so much on the king's own cultural achievements as on his generosity to artists, a generosity they acknowledge by dedicating their works to him:

quanta hodie litteras ac litteratos tum benivolentia tum liberalitate prosequaris, plurima litteratorum omnium lucubrationes tuo nomini dedicatae facile aperteque declarant.

quanto amore tu porti, quanta liberalitàte tu usi ogidì et alle lettere et alli litterati lo dimostrano apertissimamente le infinite opere di tutti li litterati al tuo nome dedicate.[115]

how much love you harbor, how much generosity you employ today for both literature and men of learning is so amply demonstrated in the countless works of all these men which are dedicated to your name.

Thus the sovereign not only holds all political-military power, but he also is the focal point of cultural activity in his kingdom. His court consists not only of collaborators and servants, commanders and soldiers, but also

---

113 Ibid., fols. 39r, 81r.

114 Paris, Bibliothèque Nationale, MS italien 616; cf. De Marinis, *La biblioteca napoletana*, 2: 131.

115 Paris, Bibliothèque Nationale, MS latin 7860, fols. 39r, 81v.

of literary men and artists that dedicate the products of their talent to him. In keeping with this picture, music was a significant presence in Naples under Ferdinand of Aragon. Besides the laudatory verses in Aurelio Brandolini's own *De laudibus musicae et Petriboni ferrariensis,* and such musical compositions as *Viva, viva rey Ferante,*[116] there was the impressive activity of Johannes Tinctoris, member of the court *cappella.* Tinctoris dedicated works of both music and music theory to Ferdinand: a Mass[117] and the two treatises *De arte contrapuncti* and *Proportionale musices.*[118] He also dedicated like fruit of his invention to Ferdinand's daughter, Beatrice: a motet[119] and the two treatises *Complexus effectuum musices* and *Terminorum musicae diffinitorium.*[120] To an outside observer (in this case Francesco Bandini, like Brandolini a Florentine in Naples and then Hungary), music in fact seemed perfectly integrated into this cultured court:

> *Se vuoi delle liberali arti exemplo egli è qui in tutta perfectione però che se o teologhi o philosophi o poeti o uomini eloquentissimi et eruditi cerchi, qui ne è assaissimi et optimi; se medici o iuristi, qui ne è in gran copia et perfecti più che in niun'altra parte d'Italia. Se musici, sculptori, pictori, architecti, ingegnieri et di simili mestieri liberali, qui ne è in tutto colmo, et del continuo la maestà del serenissimo re con ogni sollecitudine et premio attende a conducerne con continue schuole di tutte simili arti perfette.*[121]

> Should you desire an example of the liberal arts, it is here in all perfection; because if you are looking for theologians or philosophers or poets or extremely eloquent and erudite men, here they are plentiful and of the highest order; if physicians or jurists, they are here in great number, and better than in any other part of Italy. If *musicians,* sculptors, painters, architects, engineers, and those of similar liberal professions, here they are abundant, and His Most Serene Majesty continuously attends, with all solicitude and reward, to their progress with permanent schools for all such perfect arts.

116   Allan Atlas, *Music at the Aragonese Court of Naples* (Cambridge, 1985), pp. 163–66.

117   Johannes Tinctoris, *Opera omnia,* ed. William Melin (American Institute of Musicology, 1976), pp. 1–32.

118   Johannes Tinctoris, *Opera theoretica,* ed. Albert Seay (American Institute of Musicology, 1975).

119   Atlas, *Music at the Aragonese Court,* pp. 161–62.

120   Johannes Tinctoris, *Terminorum musicae diffinitorium,* ed. Peter Gülke (Kassel, 1983); and Luisa Zanoncelli, *Sulla estetica di Johannes Tinctoris: Il "Complexus effectuum musices"* (Bologna, 1979).

121   Paul O. Kristeller, "An Unpublished Description of Naples by Francesco Bandini," in *Renaissance Thoughts and Letters* (Rome, 1956), p. 408.

APPENDIX

Appendix

I

Lippi Brandoli[ni] prefatio in Libellum de laudibus musicae et Petriboni ferrariensis ad summam maiestatem regis Ferdinandi

Contemplanti mihi superioribus diebus et memoria repetenti plurimas et maximas virtutes tuas, Ferdinande rex optime, succurrit admirari te unum omnes non modo romanos, verum etiam graecos et totius orbis reges ac principes in aemulationem virtutum provocasse, adeo ut in te non immerito transferri possit ovidianum illud: "Multorum quod fuit unus heres." Nanque (ut bellicas in presentia virtutes omittamus, quibus tu cum singulis contendisti) veniebat in mentem earum virtutum cumulus quae domi atque in otio solent exerceri: prudentia, magnanimitas, modestia et, reliquarum longe maxima atque amplissima, iustitia; in quarum quidem cultu et observantia tu sine ulla dubitatione veteribus omnibus aut praestantior es aut certe non inferior. Huc accedebant bonarum artium studia liberalesque disciplinae, quas tu quidem quantum amaveris quantumque in illis profeceris (ut de reliquas taceamus) musica maximo documento est, quum nec veterum nec recentiorum principum quisquis eius rei fuerit studiosior. Quum igitur et tantarum virtutum cumulus et institutum meae professionis, praeterea quum tua in me maxima beneficia suaderent ut inciperem tandem aliquid ex meis studiis tuo nomini dedicare, placuit hoc tempore de musica potissimum aliquid tuae maiestati inscribere,

I

The preface by Lippo Brandolini to his small volume in praise of music and of Pietrobono of Ferrara, addressed to His Most High Majesty King Ferdinand

As I was musing on the days of old, and turning over in my mind your many and great virtues, Ferdinand, o best of Kings, I came to marvel how all the kings and princes, not only of Rome, but also of Greece and of the whole world, had stimulated you to imitate their virtues, to such an extent that the saying of Ovid can be fittingly applied to you: "Of the many, there was one heir." For (to omit in the present consideration the warlike virtues, in which you rival one and all) there came to my mind the array of virtues customarily exercised at home and in leisure: prudence, magnanimity, moderation, and—by far the greatest and most bountiful of all—justice; in the cultivation and practice of which you are without any doubt either superior to all the ancients or at least certainly not inferior to them. Added to this are your studies of the fine arts and the liberal disciplines: not to mention the others, music provides the best example of how much you love them and how proficient you have become in them, since not any of the ancient or modern princes has been more studious of this art. Since, therefore, both the array of such great virtues and the training of my profession, and especially, your great benefits toward me urge me to undertake at last to dedicate something from my studies to your name, I am especially pleased at this time to address to your majesty something

quod et ea res abs te ametur plurimum et esset temporibus maxime accomodata. Huic autem rei quae materiam abunde praeberet occurrit Petrusbonus ferrariensis, musicus quidem cum omnium tum vel maxime tuo iuditio praestantissimus. Nulla enim mihi videbatur aptior persona quam versibus apud te celebrari possit quam qui et in ea disciplina caeteros anteiret et abs te praeter caeteros amaretur. Accipies, igitur, ea clementia rudimenta studiorum meorum qua mihi dedisti quo id commode possem efficere ut in studiis vitam agerem; intelliges profecto hoc uno opusculo, in studiis quantum profecerim, si modo quicquid profecerim, et qualem erga tuam maiestatem animum semper habuerim atque hoc tempore habeam. Quod si ab humanitate tua impetrabo, ne hoc munusculum, qualecumque erit, recuses ac spernas, incitabis me ad maiora quottidie tuae maeistatis nomini dedicanda.

II

Ad Petrumbonum

> Inter Pieridum vates, clarissime, alumnos,
>   unica lux Phoebi, gloria summa lyrae,
> accipe parva quidem Tyrrheni munera Lippi,
>   sed tibi quam procerum nemo dedisse queat.
> 5   Sed quia nunc agimus Ferrandi munere vitam,
>   haec tibi Ferrandum mittere dona puta.
> Auratas alii vestes et pocula mittunt,
>   thesauros alii pinguiaque arva ferunt.
> Nil tamen usque manet, cunctos nil durat in annos,
> 10   nil potes ipse diu iure vocare tuum.
> Nam furto haec pereunt aut igni ususve teruntur,
>   heredum in rapidas pars venit illa manus.
> Quae vero ingenium tibi dat manuscula, Petre,
>   sola diu vivunt et tua sola diu.

about music, both because this subject is something you love greatly and because it is most timely. Regarding this subject, which offers an abundance of material, there came to mind Pietrobono of Ferrara, the musician who is the most outstanding in the judgment of all, but most importantly, in your judgment. For there did not seem to me to be any more fitting person who could be celebrated in your presence with verses than the one who both ranks ahead of the others in that discipline and is loved by you above and beyond the others. Accept, therefore, these first attempts of my studies with the same kindness with which you gave to me the wherewithal by which I could effectively manage to lead a life of study. You will surely understand from this one short work how much—if anything—I have accomplished in my studies, and with what esteem I have always regarded, and do now regard, Your Majesty. If I am successful in my request to Your Humanity that you not reject, not spurn, this small gift, whatever its quality, you will spur me on to daily accomplish greater things to dedicate to Your Majesty's name.

II

To Pietrobono

You who are most brilliant among the poets, the disciples of the Muses, O unique light of Phoebus, greatest glory of the lyre, accept the gifts of Lippo the Tuscan, small gifts, it is true, but something which no one among the great princes could have given you. Although, indeed, since now we live by the gift of Ferdinand, consider these gifts to be sent to you by Ferdinand. Some send golden fabrics and goblets, others bring treasures and rich lands. But none of these lasts, none endures through all the years, and you yourself cannot rightly call them your own for long. For some of these things are lost to the thief, or consumed by fire, or worn out by use, and the rest fall into the grasping hands of one's heirs. But these small gifts that genius gives to you, Pietro, these alone are longlasting, lastingly are yours alone.

III

Lippi Brandolini ad serenissimum regem Ferdinandum de laudibus musicae et
Petriboni libellus incipit

Huc ades ad numeros citharamque, et carmina cantus
    affer ab imparibus vecta elegia modis.
Tu quoque, dum canimus Musarum munera, Phoebe,
    huc venias, Musis sed comitate tuis.
5   Dignaque adventu sunt tot mea coepta deorum,
    digna vel in primis numine, Phoebe, tuo.
Est novus Aonidum mihi nunc dicendus alumnus,
    unica threiciae gloria honosque lyrae.
Et qui Parnasi colles ascenderit omnes,
10   non ullo fretus carminis ingenio,
nam neque Parnasum simplex via ducit ad altum
    nec soli Aonidum turba iocosa sumus.
Est tenuis vatum numerus, paucosque poetas
    bellerophontaei perficit humor equi.
15   Altera pierias aditum via praebet ad arces,
    gratior et cunctis et numerosa magis.
Haec quoque praestantes Musarum ostendit alumnos,
    unde sibi partum musica nomen habet.
Ergo, quem canimus, cursu superavit anhello,
20   ardua vix ulli culmina praessa viro.
Annue, Phebe, meis (canimus tua munera) coeptis
    et testudinem concute fila lyrae.
Incipe, tu, ductos alterno carmine versus,
    incipe, tu, laudes culta elegia novas.
25   Extulit omnipotens summo caput altus Olympo
    despexitque sua corpora facta manu.
Quumque sub hesperios aciem converteret orbes
    terrarumque caput cerneret Italiam,
artibus esse bonis ingentem vidit honorem
30   nec prolem antiquam degenerasse novam.

III

Here begins the small volume by Lippo Brandolini addressed to the Most Serene
King Ferdinand in praise of music and of Pietrobono

Come hither to my verses and my cithara, bring poems of song, carried along on mixed measures. You also, O Phoebus, come hither
while we sing of the gifts of the Muses; come hither, accompanied by
your Muses. For my undertaking is worthy of the arrival of so many   *5*
gods; above all, O Phoebus, it is worthy of your divine presence.

A new disciple of the Muses is the subject of my song, a unique
glory and honor of the Thracian lyre. And one who will ascend all
the hills of Parnassus, not confined to any one genius of song.   *10*

For no one single way leads to high Parnassus, and we are not
the only ones in the Muses' merry throng. The number of inspired
bards is slight, and Bellerophon's steed [Pegasus] produces few
full-fledged poets. Another way provides access to the citadel of the   *15*
Muses, more pleasing to all, and more melodious. This way also
boasts outstanding disciples of the Muses, and thus there has been
bestowed upon it the name Music.

Therefore the one of whom I sing has surmounted, by a strenu-   *20*
ous path, a difficult pinnacle that few men achieve.

Look with favor on my undertaking, O Phoebus (I sing of your
gifts), and touch my instrument, the strings of my lyre. Begin verses
fashioned in an elegiac poetry; begin new praises in a polished
elegy.

The omnipotent lifted his head high on Mount Olympus and   *25*
looked down on the creation made by his own hand. And when he
turned his eyes below toward the western lands and beheld Italy,
the leader of the lands, he saw that great honor was given to the
fine arts and that the ancient stock had not degenerated in the new   *30*
breed.

Quaeque rudi fuerant vero neglecta priorum
   magna ex parte novos restituisse viros.
Musica restabat, cunctis ex artibus una
   humanoque aliis gratior ingenio,
35   quam neque mortalis sat adhuc solertia nosset,
   a frygio posset nec revocare lacu.
Tum pater id damnum caelo miseratus ab alto
   non tulit hoc generi munus abesse suo.
"Ergo hominem generemus" ait "quo extincta resurgat
40   musica, quae veteres vincere possit avos."
Dixit, et eximium mira compagine corpus
   (quis credat?) manibus condidit ipse suis.
Addidit egregium robur formamque decentem,
   membraque disposuit partibus aequa suis.
45   Infuditque animam divina luce creatam,
   cui tribuit larga munera cuncta manu.
Perspicuum fortemque animum modicoque beatum
   et cultum ingenuis moribus eloquium.
Induit ingenium nullo non numine dignum,
50   Musarumque dedit munera: plectra, lyram.
"Mox age, vade, novum" dixit "te confer in orbem
   claraque sit nostro munere vita tibi.
Quicquid habet Phoebus, quicquid mea turba Camoenae
   arte sua possunt, idem damus omne tibi.
55   Denique sis Phoebus, iubeo, Phoebusque voceris;
   hoc tibi de caelo nobile nomen habe."
Dixit et hesperium iussit descendere in orbem
   qua rigat Italiae pinguia culta Padus.
Venit, adest pulchri conspectus imagine Phoebi
60   et Phoebo tantum nomine dissimilis.
Par illi forma est, par tota figura,
   caesaries ciris aemula, Phoebe, tuis.
Illum oculis vultuque refert habituque decenti,
   quaque potest alios exuperasse lyra.

Things which had previously been neglected by the crude rustic had been to a great extent restored by modern men. Only music was left lagging behind, this one art, among all the others, more pleasing to the human spirit, which human skill did not yet know *35* adequately, could not recall from the Phrygian lake.

Then our father, grieving from his high heaven that this had been lost, could not bear that this gift be lacking to his children. "Therefore let us make a man," he said, "in whom the extinct music *40* will rise again, music that will be able to surpass its ancestors of old." He spoke, and with his own hands he formed (who would believe it?) an extraordinary body of marvelous construction. He added outstanding strength and becoming form and arranged well-proportioned limbs. He infused with divine light the soul he created, and *45* bestowed upon it from his hand all great gifts: A clear, strong spirit, generously blessed, and eloquence cultivated by noble character. He clothed him with genius worthy of any god, and gave him the gifts *50* of the Muses: the plectrum, the lyre.

"Now then, go forth," he said, "devote yourself to a new world, and may an illustrious life be our gift to you. "Whatever Phoebus has, whatever my throng of Muses can do with their art, we give all the same to you. Finally, I decree that you be Phoebus, be called *55* Phoebus; have this noble name, given you from heaven." Thus he spoke, and he ordered him to go down to the land of the west, where the Po waters the fertile fields of Italy.

He came; he is here; he is seen in the image of Phoebus, differ- *60* ing from Phoebus in name only. He is like him in form, in his entire figure (with your locks, O Phoebus, vie with his dark head of hair). He takes after him in his eyes, in his face, and in his comely bearing and in that he can tower above the others in his skill with the lyre.

65   Voxque colorque idem est, eadem sunt omnia, tandem
        impositum a superis est quoque nomen idem.
    Nomen idem fuerat, sed fari nescia turba
        mutavit proprio pauca elementa sono,
    corruptoque vocat pro Phoebi nomine Petrum,
70   uno hoc grata tamen quod vocat usque Bonum.
    Ipse quidem hoc meruit, nomen tamen aptius illud
        quod sibi tu dederas, candide Phoebe, fuit.
    Aptius illud erat; quis enim tibi gratior alter,
        nominibus quis tuis dignior esse potest?
75   Namque quis hoc melior? Quisve hoc praestantior uno?
        In fidibus tanta quis movet arte manus?
    Contemplare, agedum, Musarum incensus amore
        quisquis es ante oculos singula pone tuos.
    Pende animo, citharam laeva decurrat ut omnem,
80   transigat ut celeri fila sonora manus.
    Hic digitos volitare simul miraberis omnes,
        inque locis unam tot simul esse manum.
    Nunc ruit ad summam fidium, nunc currit ad imam,
        summaque nunc digitis, nunc tenet ima lyrae.
85   Quin iures haud illi unam esse manumve lyramve,
        mille volare manus, mille sonare lyras.
    Subiice nunc animo plectro quum pulsat eburno,
        qua movet is plectrum, qua movet arte fides.
    Hic quoque praeceleres dextrae miraberis motus,
90   pulset ut ad digiti consona fila modos.
    Namque est alterius numeris obnoxia dextra
        obloquiturque omnes illius ipsa notas.
    Emicat hinc digitus, plectro micat inde sonanti
        dextera, sic peragit munus uterque suum.
95   Nec movet haec digitos, moveat nisi dextera plectrum
        nec nisi quum digitos haec movet illa fides.
    Dextera subseruit laevae, dexterae illa vicissim,
        alterius numeris altera praestat opem.

The voice, the complexion are the same, everything is the   *65*
same; finally, the same name is also bestowed upon him from
above. The name was the same, but the vulgar crowd, not knowing
how to speak, has changed a few elements with the sound of its own
language, has corrupted the name, and instead of Phoebus, calls
him Pietro, but has this to its credit, that it also calls him Good   *70*
[Bonus].

Indeed, he deserves this; still, the name that you had given
him, fair Phoebus, was more fitting. That was more fitting; for who
else was more dear to you, who can possibly be more worthy of your
names? For who is better than this man? Who is more outstanding   *75*
than this one? Who moves his hand on the strings with such art?

Come then, observe, any of you who are afire with the love of
the Muses, set before your eyes each of these things. Pay close
attention, as his left hand runs along the entire cithara, as his hand   *80*
swiftly travels along the tuneful strings. You will marvel at how all
his fingers fly simultaneously, how one hand is in so many places at
once. Now it dashes to the very top of the instrument, now it runs
to the very bottom. You would swear there could hardly be just one   *85*
hand and one lyre, but a thousand hands flying, a thousand lyres
sounding.

Attend closely now as he strikes with his ivory plectrum, see
with what art he moves the plectrum, with what art he moves the
strings. Here you will also marvel at the exceedingly swift move-
ments of his right hand, as it strikes the harmonious strings to the   *90*
rhythms of each finger.

For his right hand is obedient to the rhythms of the other; this
hand accompanies all that one's notes. His finger flashes here;
there his right hand twinkles with the sounding plectrum; thus
each fulfills its part. And this hand does not move its fingers unless   *95*
the right hand moves the plectrum, and that hand does not move
the strings except when this one moves its fingers. The right hand
complies with the left, and that, in turn, complies with the right;
each one gives its support to the rhythms of the other.

Nec datur aut plectro aut digitis spes ulla quietis,
100   est nisi perfecto carmine nulla quies.
Quos vero fidibus numeros, quae carmina plectro
    concinit? Aut quid non concinit ille lyra?
Quaecumque a Musis dilecta Britannia cantat,
    et quae non Musis Gallia grata minus,
105 quaeque gemit latis supplex Hispania terris,
    quaeque gravis concinit Italia,
denique Musarum quicquid toto extat in orbe,
    quicquid habent omnes, musica quicquid habet,
concipit hic solus plectro fidibusque canoris,
110   omnia threicia concinit ipse lyra.
At vero illa quibus numeris? Qua personat arte
    carmina? Quo vultu? Quis canit ille modis?
Hic labor, hic laus est, hic celsae gloria palmae,
    hic summum in terris musica culmen habet.
115 Aspice quam varios numeros conculcat eodem
    carmine, quas densatas contrahat arte notas.
Contrahit attenuatque notas numerosque frequentes
    et variat multis et replet usque notis.
Decurrit peragitque fides, mox rursus easdem
120   mutatis repetit terque quaterque modis.
Itque reditque lyra, vario tamen ordine semper,
    perque alios numeros itque reditque lyra.
Densentur numeri nullis in cantibus idem,
    densentur simili conditione notae.
125 Multiplicat magis atque magis turba ipsa notarum,
    quo magis hic pulsat, densa fit illa magis.
Haud alter quam quum crepitat densissima grando
    et salit assiduo tecta peruda sono,
nunc furit insano perrumpens pectine chordas
130   torrentisque modo fila per ipsa ruit.
Nunc aedit placidos lenito pectine cantus
    labitur et tactae more fluentis aquae.

And there is no hope of any rest for either plectrum or fingers,   *100*
there is no rest until the song is finished.

But what tunes does he play on his strings? what songs with his
plectrum? Rather, what does he not play on his lyre? Whatever
songs Britain sings, beloved of the Muses, and France, no less
favored by the Muses, the beseeching laments of Spain in her wide   *105*
lands, and the songs of serious Italy. Finally, whatever belongs to
the Muses throughout the whole world, whatever belongs to all of
them, whatever belongs to music, this one man produces with his
plectrum and his singing strings; he plays all of them on his   *110*
Thracean lyre.

But to what rhythms? with what art does he play his songs? with
what expression? in what modes? Here is achievement; here is
something praiseworthy; here is glory of the highest merit, here is
the high point of the world's music. Look how varied are the   *115*
rhythms he beats out to the same song, how close-packed are the
notes he executes by his art. He packs together the notes and the
crowded rhythms, and he draws them out, and he varies them and
he fills them yet again with many notes. He runs along and travels
the whole length of the strings, and immediately repeats the same   *120*
things in three or four different ways. He goes back and forth along
the lyre, but always with a different arrangement, and thus using
different rhythms he goes back and forth along the lyre. The
rhythms are not put together the same in any of his songs or the
notes put together in the same arrangement. That crowding throng   *125*
of notes grows ever greater and greater, the stronger the rhythm,
the thicker the crowd of notes. Just as when dense hail crackles and
leaps on wet roofs with unceasing sound, now he rages, pounding
the strings with a frenzied plectrum, he goes rushing along on his   *130*
instrument like a torrent. And now he gives forth quiet songs and
glides like ripples in flowing water.

Interea immotum retinet servatque tenorem,
    fidus in arte comes, fidus amore magis.
135 Illius ipse manus metatis gressibus ambas
    comprimit et certos cogit inire modos.
Ni faceret, non ullae essent in carmine leges,
    musicaque in terris maxima nulla foret.
Illius hic servat numeros, ille huius hebenis
140   flectitur, alterius sic canit alter ope.
Inchoat hic varios edocto pectine cantus
    perpetuisque canit carmina tota modis
componensque viam qua gressus dirigit ille
    metato incedit per sua fila gradu.
145 Ille iter ingreditur dextra levaque volanti,
    haec digitis plectro concinit ille levi.
Egreditur toto praescriptos carmine fines
    continuoque novos invenit ipse modos.
Impatiensque iugi superatam despicit artem,
150   hanc tamen alterius despicit artis ope.
Despicit artis opem atque artem conculcat ab arte,
    sed tamen est coepti carminis usque memor
quaque semel coepit mensuram carmine toto
    servat et ad certos itque reditque modos.
155 Metato graditur spatio finesque pererrat
    temporibusque suis ad loca certa redit.
Fine etenim modico spatiisque includitur aequis,
    stat meta haud illa praetereunda via.
Hanc habet ante oculos nullo non tempore fixam,
160   hanc fixam memori pectore semper habet.
Sed tamen hanc alia superat (quis crederet?) arte
    et velut effracto carcere liber abit.
Nunc fugit ante suum, sequitur nunc ille tenorem,
    nunc linquit proprium, nunc capit ante locum.
165 Mille habet, inque dies plures hic invenit artes,
    sed tamen in tota dedecet arte nihil.

During all this his faithful companion holds firm and maintains the unmoving tenor, a faithful companion in art, even more
faithful in love. The one restrains, with both his hands, the other's   *135*
wandering steps, and forces them to go in fixed ways. If he did not
do this, there would be no laws in song, and there would be no
great music in the world. This one maintains the rhythms of that
one; that one is swayed by this one's ebony fingerboard; thus the   *140*
music of each aids the other.

He undertakes various songs with his learned plectrum and
plays whole songs in consistent modes; and constructing the way
along which he directs his step, he sets out with measured steps
along his instrument. He sets out on his journey with left and right   *145*
hand flying, the fingers of one and the nimble plectrum of the
other working in harmony. In the whole song he goes beyond prescribed boundaries and he continually invents new modes. Impa-
tient of the yoke, he looks down on the mastered art form; he   *150*
scorns one art form, however, in aid of another. He scorns the aid
of art and walks roughshod over art by means of art, but he is
always mindful of the beginning of the song. Throughout the
whole song he maintains whatever meter he began with, and he
journeys and returns to fixed modes. Within a measured interval   *155*
he goes along and travels to the end; in his own time he returns to
fixed spots. For he is kept within the boundaries of the mode and
uniform intervals; otherwise there could hardly be such a thing as a
way to be traversed. He has this fixed before his eyes at all times; he   *160*
has this always fixed in his heart's memory. But he nevertheless
goes beyond this with another art, like one who breaks out of
prison and goes free. Now he runs ahead of his tenor, now he follows him; now he leaves his own place, now he gets there first. He   *165*
has a thousand arts, daily he invents more, but still in all his art he
does nothing unbecoming.

Cuncta facit scite, facit apto tempore cuncta,
    mille habet hinc artes, mille decenter agit.
Adde quod et vultu cantum gestumque decorat,
170   quaeque canit cithara, corpore et ore refert.
Nunc caput in terram curvat, nunc tollit in auras,
    et vultum ad citharam, labia pedesque movet.
Lumina cum fidibus flectit pariterque reflectit,
    totus cum cithara concinit ipse sua.
175 Singula quis valeat proprio describere versu?
    Haud facile est latio dicere cuncta sono.
Praeterea desunt nobis facundia vires,
    quoque hic in primis est opus eloquium.
Deficiunt ispis concinna vocabula rebus.
180   Quid multa? Ingenium linguaque deficiunt.
Tu cane pro nobis qui nosti caetera, Phoebe,
    omnia non etenim sola elegia potest.
At tu, vel totum vates celebrande per orbem,
    vates, Phoebe, gloria prima lyrae.
185 Vive, precor, felix aetas tua Nestoris annos
    expleat aut annos docta Sibylla tuos.
Utque olim vixit longum Xenophylus aevum
    musicus et nulla languit ille die.
Sic tibi nestoreos liceat vixisse per annos
190   vitaque non ullo sit temerata malo.
Te cupiant proceres, laudent regesque ducesque,
    miretur toto quisquis in orbe videt.
In primis te noster amet Ferrandus et optet,
    in primis cithara gaudeat ipse tua.
195 Huic soli studeas semper (mihi crede) placere
    solusque possis quaeque merere dabit.
Ipse viros novit virtuti praemia solus
    digna dat, hoc igitur principe vive diu.
Quumque diu felix et toto clarus in orbe
200   vixeris, ante deum consona fila move.

Know that he does all things, he does all things at the appropriate time; hence he has a thousand arts; he does a thousand things
becomingly.

Add to this that he dresses up his song with facial expression
and gesture; whatever he plays on the cithara he also presents with   *170*
his body and face. Now he bends his head to the ground, now he
lifts it to the skies, and he moves his face and his lips and his feet to
the cithara. He turns his eyes this way and that in accord with his
instrument; his whole being acts in harmony with his cithara.

Who could manage to describe each of these separate things   *175*
with its own verse? It is not even easy to speak of the whole in a
general way. Moreover, the power of speech fails us, and what is
needed most of all in this matter is eloquence. There are no adequate words for these things. What more is there to say? Genius   *180*
and language fall short. You sing for us, O Phoebus, you who
know all the rest, for indeed, elegy alone cannot do everything.

But you, O bard to be celebrated throughout the whole world,
you, O Phoebus, bard, foremost glory of the lyre, live, I pray; may   *185*
your happy lifetime fill out the years of Nestor — or your years, O
learned Sibyl. As in olden days the musician Xenophylus lived a
long life and was never sick a day, thus may it be granted to you to
have lived through Nestorian years, and may your life be unsullied
by any misfortune.   *190*

May princes desire you, kings and dukes praise you, and may
anyone in the whole world who sees you marvel. Especially may our
own Ferdinand love you and choose you; especially may he delight
in your cithara. May you always endeavor to please him alone, and   *195*
(believe me) he will give you what you alone are able to deserve.
He knows men; he alone gives worthy rewards to virtue; therefore,
long live this prince! And when you have lived a long and happy
life, famous throughout the whole world, play your tuneful strings   *200*
before God.

IV

Eiusdem de laudibus Petriboni

Orpheus auritos montes sylvasque ferasque
    dicitur ad cantus allicuisse suos,
struxisse Amphion dirceis moenia Thebis
    et murum lapides sponte adiisse sua,
5   delphinas cetasque truces vitulosque marinos
    flexit Arioniae voxque modusque lyrae.
Magna videbantur vulgo haec miracula primum,
    sed docuit Petrus haec Bonus esse nihil.
Ille artem numerosque omnes ita callet, ut ipsum,
10   si liceat, Phoebum vel superare queat.
Sive leves digitos plectrumque volatile chordis
    admovet et tota fertque refertque lyra,
Seu gallos peragit numeros, numerosque britannos,
    hesperios gemitus, italicosque modos.
15   Orpheane et sylvas flexisse et Ariona pisces
    saxaque dirceum credis? Iniquus homo es.
Rustica mulcebant indocto pectora cantu
    insuetumque novis artibus ingenium.
Credula simplicitas grata novitate retenta est
20   et capitur modica sensus ab arte rudis.
Hinc fama est motos venisse ad carmina montes
    et murum lapides insiliisse novum.
At Petrus cithara proceres regesque peritos
    inque illa eximios detinet ante viros.
25   Rustica corda parum est modico deflectere cantu,
    qui flectit doctos, hic mihi doctus erit.

IV

By the same author, in praise of Pietrobono

Orpheus is said to have attracted the listening mountains and
forests and wild beasts to his songs; it is said that Amphion built the
walls of Boeothian Thebes, and stones came to the wall of their
own accord, the sound and music of Arion's lyre swayed dolphins   *5*
and savage sea-beasts and seals.

   These seemed to the common folk of olden days to be great
miracles, but Pietrobono has taught us that this is nothing. He himself is so skilled in his art and in all rhythms that he could vanquish   *10*
Phoebus himself if that were allowed. He moves his nimble fingers
and his plectrum that flies along the strings, and he goes back and
forth along the whole lyre; he performs French songs and British,
Spanish laments and Italian melodies.

   Do you believe that Orpheus moved forests, and Arion fish,   *15*
and the Theban rocks? You are a wicked person. They stirred with
their crude music the hearts of rustics, and with their novel arts
those whose minds were not used to such things. Credulous simplicity is enthralled by pleasing novelty, and uncultured sensitivity is   *20*
captivated by a middling art. From this comes the legend that
mountains were moved and came to the songs, that stones leaped
into a new wall.

   But Pietro with his cithara captivates princes and kings who are
experts, and with it also men who are already exceptionally skilled.
It is not enough to move untutored hearts with middling song; he   *25*
who sways the learned, this is the one who in my eyes is learned.

V

Eiusdem ad Ferdinandum regem

> Inclyta progenies regum regumque vicissim
>   magne pater, italo rex venerande solo.
> Gesisti tu cuncta quidem prudenter et actum est
>   ante tibi hac summo nil sine consilio.
> 5   Nil tamen hoc unquam gestum prudentius uno est
>   quum Petrum accisti sub tuo iure Bonum.
> Si licet, hic unus Dircaeum et Ariona vincit
>   Orpheaque et Phoebo te, Line clare, tuo.
> Gloria pellaeum concisse ad praelia cantu,
> 10   summa fuit titulis, Timothee, tuis.
> Hic trahit a bellis summos ad carmina reges,
>   doctior hic armis, nam toga docta magis.
> Haud alia tu dignus eras, rex maxime, musa:
>   hic quo non alio te nisi dignus erat.
> 15   Praestantes optas, nam praestantissimus ipse es:
>   coniunctos paribus sic decet esse pares.
> Hunc nosti solus, solus te novit et ipse,
>   hunc tu si sapies haud procul ire sines.
> Sed facies puto, iamque facis, quid vana movemus?
> 20   Nunc, nunc vix dicam, rex mihi magne, sapis.

VI

Eiusdem ad libellum ut Ferdinandum adeat

> Vade, age, parve liber, celsam te confer in arcem
>   et pete Ferrandi limina clara dulcis.
> Ante fores sistas, studio te protinus omni
>   Maecenas quaerit suscipitque tuus.
> 5   Admittetque meas captato tempore nugas
>   et dabit optata principis aure frui.
> Te legit, esto brevis, brevibus favet ille libellis,
>   mox illi haec nostro nomine pauca refer:

V

By the same author, to King Ferdinand

O splendid descendant of kings and in turn the great father of kings, venerable king of the Italian land: indeed you have done all things prudently, and nothing has yet been done by you without the most excellent judgment. But no deed was ever more prudent 5 than this: to take Pietrobono under your jurisdiction.

If such a thing is permissible, this one individual vanquishes the Dircaean [Amphion], and Arion, and Orpheus, and you, fair Linus, are surpassed by your Phoebus. Having incited Alexander to battle by your song is the supreme glory to your credit, O Timo- 10 theus. This man draws great kings away from wars to his songs; he is more learned than arms, for the toga is the more learned.

It would hardly have been worthy of you, O greatest king, to have any other Muse: this one was worthy of no one other than you. You choose those who are outstanding because you yourself are the 15 most outstanding; it is fitting that equals be thus joined to equals. You alone know him and he alone knows you; if you are wise you will surely not allow him to go far away.

But I think you will do this, and indeed are already doing it; 20 why am I wasting my breath? Now, now let me just say that you, O my great king, are wise.

VI

By the same author, to his little book, exhorting it to go to Ferdinand

Go now, little book, betake yourself to the high hill, and seek the illustrious dwelling of our sweet Ferdinand. Set yourself before his doors; with all diligence your Maecenas seeks you and receives you immediately. At that eagerly awaited moment, he will admit my tri- 5 fles, and give them to the ear of the prince, which I have sought, for his enjoyment. He reads you, be brief, he is partial to brief little books; quickly bring to him these few words in our name:

"Maxime rex, si fas magnis dare munera parva,

10   haec tibi dat Lippus munera parva tuus.

Dat mentem, non munus inops dat carmina vates,

     carmine nil maius quod dare possit habet.

Dat quoque parva tibi, ne tu sibi magna remittas,

     nam qui magna ferant munera, magna petunt.

15   Haud igitur vultu nunc accipe parva sereno,

     aut quum magna feret magna referre para."

"O greatest king, if it is permissible to give small gifts to the
great, your Lippo gives these small gifts to you. He gives his mind,   *10*
the bard gives his songs, no beggarly gift; he has nothing that he
could give you that is greater than song. And he gives you small
things, so that you won't give him great things in return, for those
who bring great gifts are asking for great returns. Now, therefore,   *15*
accept small things with a serene countenance, or else be ready
when he brings great things to give equally great things in return."

Index